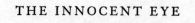

THE INNOCENT EYE

THE
INNOCENT
EYE

HERBERT READ

NEW YORK: HENRY HOLT AND COMPANY

PRINTED IN THE UNITED STATES OF AMERICA

CONTENTS

PART I
THE INNOCENT EYE
I

PART II

THE FALCON AND THE DOVE
59

PART III

THE ADAMANTINE SICKLE
251

PREFACE

Lern im Leben die Kunst, im Kunstwerk lerne das Leben,
Siehst du das Eine recht, siehst du das andere auch.

HÖLDERLIN

THE OUTBREAK of another war, with a consequent suspension of normal activities, gave me the impulse and the opportunity to continue the narrative which I began ten years ago in "The Innocent Eye." The contrast between that early idyllic prelude and the confused experience of the years which followed might, I thought, be of more than personal interest, and provide the material for some moral generalizations external to the narrative. I have tried to be honest with my evidence, and it is for others to pass a verdict. My story—which is deliberately a story of the mind —is the story of an idealist confronted with the possibility of despair, of a romantic condemned to the incidence of bleak realities. What value it may have seems to me as the narrator to be due to the fact that in spite of a disillusion which is at once personal and universal, I persist in a simple faith in the natural goodness of man. These pages will make sufficiently clear that I consider the no-man's-years between the wars as largely futile, spent unprofitably by me and all my kind. I do not pretend to know how we could have

PREFACE

made them more positive: the forces against us were not human, but satanic—blind forces of economic drift, with the walls of faith and reason turning to air behind us. But at some future date men will desire to be more omniscient, and these annals may then fill an otherwise empty page, contributing their jot to the final judgment.

The events of these years have frustrated our intellectual plans, exceeded the limits of art, and thrown us back on the elementary foundations of philosophy. If I now turn tentatively to the East, it is not in any spirit of eclecticism. The necessary renewal of faith in life must come from deep sources—sources as deep as those from which Christianity itself once flowed. These are only Eastern and apparently exotic because the East is ancient, and we are modern and immature. Our crisis is not, as superficial observers are always telling us, an end crisis—the last stages of decay. On the contrary, it is a crisis of adolescence, of a young world that must now break through the parent-bondage and test its own independent virility. This universal psychosis will not kill our civilization: but it can only be cured by a communal effort of will for which history offers no precedent. In other words, our need is creative action on a new scale—to be more exact, on a supernational scale. But the supernational is simply the human, and only a faith in the human, as a culmination of natural law and of creative evolution, will suffice.

This book will attempt to show how I have come to believe that the highest manifestation of the immanent will of the universe is the work of art. I have found that the experience of art leads back to the natural law: a truth expressed by the

PREFACE

great poet whose epigram I have put at the head of this Preface. I would like to conclude on a less solemn note, and turn to a great philosopher who renounced poetry, even the poetry of life, in order to be perfectly detached. Though my book is not what is normally regarded as a confession, and offers none of the inducements to a reader conveyed by the word confession, yet the writing of it has been in some sense an alleviation of dread. For this reason I can say with Kierkegaard that "it is only after a man has thus understood himself inwardly, and has thus seen his way, that life acquires peace and significance; only then is he rid of that tiresome, ill-omened fellow-traveller, the irony of life."

H. R.

PART I

THE
INNOCENT EYE

Potential
mirror of gentle acts
agent of factual
joy

enjoy
deft engines
but shade yourself
against electric signs

that in the night
destroy the stars
and lurid phantoms
feature on hotel stairs.

Angelicos,
diatoms
of senseful surfeit—
How can man deny you?

He should employ you
whenever
He wakes in the world
out of dusty fever

and with not worm
and weevil
for whom
God grows stavesacre

but with bird and lynx
enlarge his life
with crystal lens
and furtive lust.

I

THE VALE

WHEN I went to school I learned that the Vale in which we lived had once been a lake, but long ago the sea had eaten through the hills in the east and so released the fresh waters, leaving a fertile plain. But such an idea would have seemed strange to my innocent mind, so remote was this menacing sea. Our farm was towards the western end of the Vale, and because all our land was as flat as once the surface of the lake had been, we could see around us the misty hills, the Moors to the north, the Wolds to the south, meeting dimly in the east where they were more distant. This rim of hills was nearest in the south, at least in effect; for as the sun sank in the west the windows of Stamper's farm in the south caught the blazing rays and cast them back at us, continually drawing our eyes in that direction. But we never traveled so far south as those hills; for the Church and the Market, the only outer places of pilgrimage, lay to the north, five or six miles away. By habit we faced north: the south was 'behind.'

I seemed to live, therefore, in a basin, wide and shallow like the milkpans in the dairy; but the even bed of it was checkered with pastures and cornfields, and the rims were the soft blues and purples of the moorlands. This basin was my world, and I had no inkling of any larger world, for no strangers came to us out of it, and we never went into it. Very rarely my Father went to York or Northallerton, to buy a piece of machinery for the farm or to serve on a jury at the Assizes; but only our vague wonder accompanied him, and the toys he brought back with him might have come, like sailors' curios, from Arabia or Cathay. The basin at times was very wide, especially in the clearness of a summer's day; but as dusk fell it would suddenly contract, the misty hills would draw near, and with night they had clasped us close: the center of the world had become a candle shining from the kitchen window. Inside, in the sitting-room where we spent most of our life, a lamp was lit, with a round glass shade like a full yellow moon. There we were bathed before the fire, said our prayers kneeling on the hearthrug, and then disappeared up the steep stairs lighted by a candle to bed; and once there, the world was finally blotted out. I think it returned with the same suddenness, at least in Summer; but the waking world was a new world, a hollow cube with light streaming in from one window across to a large bed holding, as the years went by, first one, then two, and finally three boys, overseen by two Apostles from one wall and adjured from another, above a chest of drawers, by a white pottery plaque within a pink-luster frame, printed with a vignette of an angel blowing a trumpet and the words:

PRAISE YE THE LORD.

Sometimes the child's mind went on living even during the darkness of night, listening to the velvet stillness of the

6

fields. The stillness of a sleeping town, of a village, is nothing to the stillness of a remote farm; for the peace of day in such a place is so kindly that the ear is attuned to the subtlest sounds, and time is slow. If by chance a cow should low in the night it is like the abysmal cry of some hellish beast, bringing woe to the world. And who knows what hellish beasts might roam by night, for in the cave by the Church five miles away they once found the bones of many strange animals, wolves and hyenas, and even the tusks of mammoths. The night-sound that still echoes in my mind, however, is not of this kind: it is gentler and more musical —the distant sound of horse-hooves on the highroad, at first dim and uncertain, but growing louder until they more suddenly cease. To that distant sound, I realized later, I must have come into the world, for the Doctor arrived on horseback at four o'clock one December morning to find me uttering my first shriek.

I think I heard those hooves again the night my father died, but of this I am not certain; perhaps I shall remember when I come to relate that event, for now the memory of those years, which end shortly after my tenth birthday, comes fitfully, when the proper associations are aroused. If only I can recover the sense and uncertainty of those innocent years, years in which we seemed not so much to live as to be lived by forces outside us, by the wind and trees and moving clouds and all the mobile engines of our expanding world—then I am convinced I shall possess a key to much that has happened to me in this other world of conscious living. The echoes of my life which I find in my early childhood are too many to be dismissed as vain coincidences; but it is perhaps my conscious life which is the echo, the only real experiences in life being those lived with a virgin sensibility—so that we only hear a tone once, only see a color once, see, hear, touch, taste and smell everything but once, the first time. All life is an echo of our first sensations, and we build up our consciousness, our whole mental life, by variations and combinations of these elementary sensations. But it is more complicated than that, for the senses apprehended not only colors and tones and shapes, but also patterns and atmosphere, and our first discovery of these determines the larger patterns and subtler atmospheres of all our subsequent existence.

2

THE FARM

I HAVE given the impression that the Farm was remote, but this is not strictly true. Not half a mile on each side of us was another farmhouse, and clustering near the one to the east were three or four cottages. We formed, therefore, a little community, remote as such; in Doomsday Book we had been described as a hamlet. The nearest village was two or three miles away, but to the south, so that it did not count for much until we began to go to school, which was not until towards the end of the period of which I write. Northwards our farm road ran through two fields and then joined the highroad running east and west; but eastward this road soon turned into a road running north and south, down which we turned northwards again, to the Church five miles away, and to Kirby, our real metropolis, six miles away.

The farmhouse was a square stone box with a roof of vivid red tiles; its front was to the south, and warm enough to shelter some apricot trees against the wall. But there was no traffic that way: all our exits and entrances were made on the north side, through the kitchen; and I think even our grandest visitors did not disdain that approach. Why

9

should they? On the left as they entered direct into the kitchen was an old oak dresser; on the right a large open fireplace, with a great iron kettle hanging from the reckan, and an oven to the near side of it. A long deal table, glistening with a honey gold sheen from much scrubbing, filled the far side of the room; long benches ran down each side of it. The floor was flagged with stone, each stone neatly outlined with a border of some softer yellow stone, rubbed on after every washing. Sides of bacon and plum dusky hams hung from the beams of the wooden ceiling.

By day it was the scene of intense bustle. The kitchen-maid was down by five o'clock to light the fire; the laborers crept down in stockinged feet and drew on their heavy boots; they lit candles in their horn lanthorns and went out to the cattle. Breakfast was at seven, dinner at twelve, tea at five. Each morning of the week had its appropriate activity: Monday was washing day, Tuesday ironing, Wednesday and Saturday baking, Thursday 'turning out' upstairs and churning, Friday 'turning out' downstairs. Every day there was the milk to skim in the dairy—the dairy was to the left of the kitchen, and as big as any other room in the house. The milk was poured into large flat pans and allowed to settle; it was skimmed with horn scoops, like toothless combs.

At dinner, according to the time of the year, there would be from five to seven farm laborers, the two servant girls, and the family, with whom, for most of the time, there was a governess—a total of from ten to fifteen mouths to feed every day. The bustle reached its height about midday; the men would come in and sit on the dresser, swinging their legs impatiently; when the food was served, they sprang to the benches and ate in solid gusto, like animals. They disappeared as soon as the pudding had been served, some to smoke a pipe in the saddle room, others to do work which could not wait. Then all the clatter of washing up rose and subsided. More peaceful occupations filled the afternoon. The crickets began to sing in the hearth. The kettle boiled for tea. At nightfall a candle was lit, the foreman or the shepherd sat smoking in the armchair at the fireside end of the table. The latch clicked as the others came in one by one and went early to bed.

The kitchen was the scene of many events which afterwards flowed into my mind from the pages of books. Whenever in a tale a belated traveler saw a light and came through the darkness to ask for shelter, it was to this kitchen door. I can no longer identify the particular stories, but they do not belong to this period of childhood so much as to my later boyhood and youth, long after I had left the Farm; and even today my first memories easily usurp the function of the imagination, and clothe in familiar dimensions and patterns, exact and objective, the scenes which the romancer has purposely left vague. Perhaps the effect of all romance depends on this faculty we have of giving our own definition to the fancies of others. A mind without memories means a body without sensibility; our memories make our imaginative life, and it is only as we increase our memories, widening the imbricated shutters which divide our mind from the light, that we find with quick recognition those images of truth which the world is pleased to attribute to our creative gift.

3

THE GREEN

THE Green, a space of about an acre, lay in front of the
kitchen door. It was square; one side, that to the left
as we came out of the house, was fully taken up by a range
of sheds. A shorter range of buildings continued in line with
the house on the right—first the saddle-room, one of my
favorite haunts, then the shed where the dog-cart and
buggy were kept, and finally the blacksmith's shop. Beyond
this were the grindstones and the ash-heap (in just such a
heap, I imagined, Madame Curie discovered radium) and
then a high hedge led to the corner of the Green, where
three enormous elm-trees, the only landmark near our farm,
overhung the duck-pond. On the other two sides the Green
was bounded by hedges. The farm-road led past the sheds
and then to the left through the stackyard; to the right there
was a cart-track leading across the fields to the next farm
with its cluster of cottages.

Our dominion was really four-fold: the Green I have just
described, and then three other almost equal squares, the
one to the left of the Green being the farm outhouses, a
rectangular court of low buildings enclosing the Fodgarth,
or Foldgarth, and two others to the south of the house, the

orchard to the east, the garden to the west. Each province was perfectly distinct, divided off by high walls or hedges; and each had its individual powers or mysteries. The Green was the province of water and of fowl, of traffic and trade, the only province familiar to strangers—to the postman and the pedlar, and the scarlet huntsmen. In Winter we made the snowman there; in Summer avoided its shelterless waste. On Mondays the washed clothes flapped in the wind, but for the rest of the week it was willingly resigned to hens, ducks, geese, guinea fowls, and turkeys—whose discursive habits, incidentally, made it no fit playground for children. The pond was more attractive, but because of its stagnation it could not compete with the becks not far away. I remember it best in a hot Summer, when the water dried up and left a surface of shining mud, as smooth as moleskin, from which projected the rusty wrecks of old cans and discarded implements. Perhaps it was a forbidden area; it serves no purpose in my memory.

The pump was built over a deep well, in the corner of the Green near the kitchen; it was too difficult for a boy to work. One day, underneath the stones which took the drip, we discovered bright green lizards. Behind the pump, handy to the water, was the copper-house—the 'copper' being a large cauldron built in over a furnace. Here the clothes were boiled on a Monday; here, too, potatoes for the pigs were boiled in their earthy skins, and the pigs were not the only little animals who enjoyed them, for they are delicious when cooked in this way. Outside the same copper-house the pigs were killed, to be near the cauldron of boiling water with which they were scalded. The animal was drawn from its sty by a rope through the ring in its nose: its squealing filled the whole farm till it reached the copper-house, and there by the side of a trestle its throat was cut with a sharp knife and the hot blood gushed on to the ground. The carcass was then stretched on the trestle, and the whole household joined in the work of scraping the scalded hide: it was done with metal candlesticks, the hollow foot making a sharp and effective instrument for removing the bristles and outer skin. The carcass was then disemboweled and dismembered. The copper was once more requisitioned to render down the superfluous fat, which was first cut into dices. The remnants of this process, crisp shreds known as scraps, formed our favorite food for days afterwards. In fact, pig-killing was followed by a whole orgy of good things to eat—pork-pies, sausages and pigs'-feet filling the bill for a season. But the scenes I have described, and many others of the same nature, such as the searing of horses' tails, the killing of poultry, the birth of cattle, even the lewdness of a half-witted laborer, were witnessed by us children with complete passivity—just as I have seen children of the same age watching a bull-fight in Spain quite unmoved by its horrors. Pity, and even terror, are emotions which develop when we are no longer innocent, and the sentimental adult who induces such emotions in the child is probably breaking through defenses which nature has wisely put round the tender mind. The child even has a natural craving for horrors. He survives just because he is without sentiment, for only in this way can his green heart harden sufficiently to withstand the wounds that wait for it.

On the south side of the Green were two familiar shrines,

each with its sacred fire. The first was the saddle-room, with its pungent clean smell of saddle-soap. It was a small white-washed room, hung with bright bits and stirrups and long loops of leather reins; the saddles were in a loft above, reached by a ladder and trap-door. In the middle was a small cylindrical stove, kept burning through the Winter, and making a warm friendly shelter where we could play undisturbed. Our chief joy was to make lead shot, or bullets as we called them; and for this purpose there existed a long-handled crucible and a mold. At what now seems to me an incredibly early age we melted down the strips of lead we found in the window-sill, and poured the sullen liquid into the small aperture of the mold, which was in the form of a pair of pincers—closed whilst the pouring was in progress. When opened, the gleaming silver bullets, about the size of a pea, fell out of the matrix and rolled away to cool on the stone floor. We used the bullets in our catapults, but the joy was in the making of them, and in the sight of their shining beauty.

The blacksmith's shop was a still more magical shrine. The blacksmith came for a day periodically, to shoe or re-shoe the horses, to repair wagons and make simple implements. In his dusky cave the bellows roared, the fire was blown to a white intensity, and then suddenly the bellows-shaft was released and the soft glowing iron drawn from the heart of the fire. Then clang, clang, clang on the anvil, the heavenly shower of ruby and golden sparks, and our precipitate flight to a place of safety. All around us, in dark cobwebbed corners, were heaps of old iron, discarded horse-shoes, hoops and pipes. Under the window was a tank of water for slaking and tempering the hot iron, and this water possessed the miraculous property of curing warts.

In these two shrines I first experienced the joy of making things. Everywhere around me the earth was stirring with growth and the beasts were propagating their kind. But these wonders passed unobserved by my childish mind, unrecorded in memory. They depended on forces beyond our control, beyond my conception. But fire was real, and so was the skill with which we shaped hard metals to our design and desire.

4

THE ORCHARD

THE front garden was formal, like the drawing-room; it was not part of our customary world. If we went there during the day, it was to see if the forbidden apricots were ripening, or to play for a short time round the monkey-puzzle-tree which grew in the middle of a small lawn. But a monkey-puzzle-tree is not a friendly shelter; its boughs are too near the ground, it is hirsute and prickly. The lawn was enclosed by hedges of box, through which narrow arches led to the flower garden in front, to the vegetable garden on the right, and to the orchard on the left. Again, all these provinces were rectangular, without any picturesque charm, but riotous with natural detail, with great variety of shrubs, fruit-bushes and vegetables. The Garden, too, had its shrine. The northern end, in line with the back of the house, was bounded by a high stone wall, sheltering pear-trees. Between this wall and a line of plum-trees, a path, bordered by flowering-currants and honesty, led to the ivy-clad privy. This green retreat, always in memory a place spangled in leaf-flecked sunlight, with ivy-fruit tapping against the small window-pane, has no grosser associations. Its friendliness, its invitation to sociability, was further emphasized by its furniture of two seats, and there we could sit side by side, the needs of our bodies relieved in no furtive secrecy, but in unabashed naturalness.

On the other side, through the wicket that led into the Orchard, there came first the water-trough, an immense stone tank fed from the eaves; this rain water was very precious for washing purposes, so we were forbidden to play with it. It is one of the few memories I have of the sternness of my Father, that on one occasion finding me transgressing this law, he immediately picked me up by the seat and immersed me bodily in the water.

Above the trough, high up on the gable of the house, was another forbidden object: the bell which was pealed at midday to announce dinner to the scattered laborers, none of whom was likely to wear a watch.

Behind the saddle-room, in this region of the trough, was the Sand-heap, in a corner formed by a lime house and a low cow-shed. The hours we spent in this corner were too habitual to linger much in the memory. It was a generous heap, allowing an extensive system of trenches and castles; near-by was the shade of the apple-trees and the elms; our days there were timeless. Once, playing there, I slipped into the cow-shed to stroke a young calf housed there, closing the door behind me. The calf was lying in fresh clean straw, and did not stir at my approach. Hours later I was missed, and after long searching and much shouting in the farm and the fields, I was discovered sleeping with my head against the calf's warm flank.

The Orchard, like the Green, must have been about an acre in extent. I have no memory of it, except in Spring and

Summer, when the branches, with their succession of blossom, leaf and fruit, met to form an overgrowth supported by aisles of trunks, green with moss or misty gray-blue when the lichen was dry and crusted. One old russet tree sloped up from the ground at a low angle, easy to climb; and in its boughs we shook the blossom till it fell in flakes like snow, or helped ourselves unchecked to the sweet rough-skinned apples. I think the Orchard only held two treasures besides the trees: an old disused roller about which we clambered, and in a far corner, by a bush whose hollow twigs made excellent stems for improvised pipes (in which we smoked a cunning mixture of dried clover and pear leaves), a small trough which usually held rock salt, brown and glassy. In the orchard, and in the paddock beyond, we dug up sweet pig-nuts, and ate them without much regard for the soil engrained in them.

When we emerged from the Paddock, where our pony and the mare for the dog-cart used to graze, there was a sudden sense of space. The ground sloped down gently towards our main stream, the Riccall, which formed the southern boundary of the farm. Beyond the Riccall, which flowed rather deeply in the soft earth and was quite impassable to us, lay a mysterious land we never explored: the south, with the hills rising in the distance, the farm with the fiery windows hidden in their folds.

5

THE FOLDGARTH

THE fourth kingdom, the Foldgarth, was the animal kingdom. We usually entered it from the north corner of the Green, and here on the right were the main cowsheds, the most familiar part of this complex of buildings. Morning and night, and most often by lanthorn light (perhaps it is only the Winter scene which is impressed on my memory) the cows were milked in a glow and atmosphere which is for me the glow and atmosphere of the Nativity. The patient beasts stood in their stalls, exuding the soft slightly sickly smell of cow breath; a girl or a man sat on a three-legged stool, cheek against a glossy flank, and the warm needle stream of milk hissed into the gleaming pails. At first it sang against the hollow tin drum of the base, but as the pail filled it murmured with a frothy surr-surr. Here I learned my first bitter lesson of self-limitations; for try as I would I could not learn how to milk. To manipulate the teats so as to secure a swift and easy flow of milk demands a particular skill; I never acquired it, though my brothers, younger than I, seemed to find no difficulty. This was my first humiliation in the practical affairs of life; another which I might mention here was an inability to make the kuk-kuk noise between the tongue and palate which is the proper sound to urge a horse on gently. These failures in trivial things loom much larger in childhood and affect us much more deeply than any backwardness in learning manners or facts, for they reflect on our physical capacity, and that is much more real to us than any mental power.

Then, along the northern side of the Foldgarth, ran the stable for the carthorses. We were a little scared of these immense noble beasts, for some of them were known to be savage, and ready to bite anyone but the man whose duty it was to look after them. At the end of the stables a gateway led into the stackyard, and so out on to the road and the fields beyond. At this gateway I once witnessed a terrible scene; an ignorant laborer had taken a pregnant mare out to plow, and by overstraining her, caused a miscarriage. My Father and I met him bringing in the horse, with her ghastly trail, and so terrible was my Father's passion that he quite forgot my presence as he heaped his curses on the offending man.

My memories of my Father are too intermittent to form a coherent image. His sensitive face, his soft brown eyes, and his close curly black hair were not the features of a normal farmer. He loved his Farm and was well known for his fervor and enterprise, a tradition he had inherited from my Grandfather: he brought some visionary quality to his life and labor. He was a man of austere habits and general uprightness, whose friendship was sought by men of a more recognized intellectual standing. Yet I do not remember that he read much or was in any sense bookish (as I shall relate later, books were scarce in the house). The life of a farmer is hardly consistent with a life of even elementary scholarship, but a sensitive and intelligent mind, in daily contact with all the problems and processes of farming, acquires more than a weather wisdom—an intuitive sense of reality and right values which are not acquired by the mere process of reading.

Along the western side of the Foldgarth ran a line of higher, double-storied buildings. The first was a big hay-barn, open to the rafters, with the pigeon-house built in at the gable end. It was a favorite playing-ground in wet weather: we could make giddy leaps from one level of hay to another; we could burrow into caves and hide completely in its scented warmth. A door at the other side of this barn led to a circular building, with a grinding mill in the middle and a circular track round which a horse could drag the mill-beam.

Then came various sheds for fodder and implements, and over these, approached by stone steps at the end of the building, and outside the Foldgarth, was the granary—a long dry sweet-smelling loft, with bins of golden wheat and stacks of oil-cake, and a store of locust-beans which we ate when we were hungry. A machine for crushing oil-cake stood against one wall, and in this one day I managed to crush my little finger. I fainted with the pain, and the horror of that dim milk-white panic is as ineffaceable as the scar which my flesh still bears.

The other two sides of the Foldgarth were occupied by pig-sties and cow-sheds; the middle by a steadily steaming morass of urine-sodden straw known as the Mig Heap, the infinitely precious store of manure from which the land recovered some of the strength given forth in corn and pasture. The acrid stench of this heap, never unpleasant to any one brought up with it, pervaded the whole of the Foldgarth. The pigeons flocked from roof to roof. An inquisitive calf would lift its head over the low door of its stall. A scurry of hens, an occasional grunt or squeal of pigs, the running of a rope through a ring in the stables: these were the only sounds that disturbed the day's peace, until the men returned from the fields with the weary horses, and the Foldgarth was filled with the clatter of hooves on the stone sets, with the whistling and hissing of the men over their grooming.

On the southern side of the Foldgarth, some of the stables opened outwards, into a lane whose other side was the high wall on the north of the vegetable garden. Here lived the hunters, beautiful pedigree horses which were the pride of the Farm—lived in a cleanliness and comfort which put them in a class apart, half-way between humans and animals. I fancy that the fortunes of the Farm depended far more on these splendid pampered darlings than on the normal crops and cattle. It was a great day when they were paraded in all their glossy splendor before some horse-dealer, and a bargain struck. But sorrow must have been mingled with satisfaction when they left us, and a farm is, indeed, the scene of many sad farewells: pet lambs and ducks stolen away to go to the market with the rest, leaving a broken-hearted child to weep the day away until some consolation is found.

THE STACKYARD

BEYOND the Foldgarth lay the Stackyard, looking like an African village, especially after the harvest when it was stored to its limits. The stacks were of two shapes—circular and rectangular—with swelling sides and neatly thatched roofs. The ridges of the rectangular ones were braided with osiers; the round ones were finished off with a fanciful panache of straw. Birds sheltered under the narrow eaves, and would dart out at our strident approach. One Summer evening something not bird nor bat fluttered among the stacks; the farm was roused to excitement and the winged creature finally netted. It was a rare Death's Head moth, for which some collector paid the fabulous sum of five shillings. That such riches could lurk in a stackyard was a new portent. We learned that the Death's Head moth was fond of the potato-flower, and the season never afterwards passed without a vain hunt among these despised blooms.

The great festival in the Stackyard was threshing time. Late one afternoon we would hear the chuff and rattle of the engine and threshing machine far away on the high-road, and away we would race to meet it. The owner of the engine, Jabez by name, was a great hero in the eyes of children. He was a small man with a little twinkling face and a fuzzy black beard. He would stop his rattling train and take us up into the engine cabin. I love to this day that particular smell of hot steam and oil which was then wafted to us. With amazement we watched Jabez push over his levers and set the monster in motion. With more chuffing and much complicated shunting the machines were steered into position for work, and then left shrouded for the night.

Very early the next morning we would hear a high-pitched musical hum coming from the Stackyard, and it was with difficulty that we could be made to eat any breakfast. Then we would run across the Green and find round the corner the most exciting scene of the year. The engine stood before us, merry with smoke and steam; the big fly-wheel winked in the sunlight; the bright balls of the revolving 'governor' (Jabez had taught me the technical names) twinkled in a minor radiance. Jabez was in the cabin stoking the glowing furnace. The big leather belt swung rhythmically between the fly-wheel and the threshing-machine. Two men on the top of a stack threw down the sheaves; two others cut them open and guided them into the monster's belly; the monster groaned and gobbled, and out of its yammering mouth came the distracted straw; elsewhere emerged the prickly chaff and below, into sacks that reached the ground, trickled the precious corn. A cloud of dust and chaff swirled round everything. As the stack disappeared, and approached ground-level, we were armed with sticks and the dogs became attentive and expectant. The last layer of sheaves was reached; out raced the rats which had made a home in the bedding of thorns on which the stack rested, and then for a few minutes the Stackyard was an abode of demons: dogs barked, men and children shouted in a lust of killing, and the unfortunate rats squealed in panic and death agonies. Sometimes we found a nest of newly-born rats, and then we were suddenly sad.

I think this festival used to last two or three days; it was our only contact with the Machine God. I suppose we were dimly aware of the railway six miles away, and must have traveled on it, for I know that once or twice we went to Scarborough; but for some reason I have no vivid memory of these excursions, nor of anything associated with them. They were not lived, but pushed without roots into the soil of our daily existence. One curious experience, however, remains with me, and it may well be mentioned here; it is the first of several instances in my life of which I remain incapable of asserting that the experience was of the dream-world. My reason tells me, in this case at least, that it must have been a dream, but the mind does not necessarily assent to its reasoning. I 'appeared' (as we say) to walk down the cart-track that led along the top side of two or three fields towards Peacock's farm; I climbed on to the gate that separated the last field from the high-road, and as I rested there I was terrified by the sudden onrush of a large steam roller, traveling northwards. It was distinguished from ordinary steam-rollers (which I had no doubt seen at work on the roads) by the fact that the boiler rested on an enormous bellows, and as the engine roared onwards, these bellows worked up and down and so seemed to throw up through the chimney a fiery column of smoke, steam and sparks.

26

THE STACKYARD

This apparition, which came to me perhaps in my seventh year, remains in my mind today distinct in every detail.

I do not think I was more than usually subject to nightmares (if such this was), but one, which I fancy belongs to a common form, is also remembered by me with peculiar vividness, though it is difficult to describe. I am laid as in bed on a bank of clouds. The sky darkens, grows bluish-black. Then the darkness seems to take visible shape, to separate into long bolsters, or object which I should now compare with airships. These then point themselves towards me, and approach me, magnifying themselves enormously as they get nearer. I awake with a shriek, quivering with terror. My Mother hears me and comes quickly to comfort me, perhaps to take me back with her to sleep away the sudden terror.

7

THE COW PASTURE

THERE was a sandy rankness about the fields stretch-
ing towards the river, but these were the main pasture-
lands. The Cow Pasture, by far the largest field on the
farm, lay on the west of the farm-buildings and its boundary
was the western boundary of our land. A path led across
the middle of it, and across the neighboring fields to Riccall
House, distinguished from the rest of us by its white-washed
walls and thatched roof. This pasture was rather a godless
waste: it was pock-marked with erupted rabbit-warrens,
countless mole-hills, and dark fairy-rings in the grass. We
implicitly believed in the mysterious origin of these rings,
and felt that we might any misty morning find the fairies
dancing. Periodically the rabbits had to be decimated, and
then fierce dark men with waxed mustaches appeared,
bringing ferrets in canvas bags. We would go out in a party,
carrying guns and spades, to attack the warrens. The ferrets
were loosened from their bags and disappeared down the
holes. We listened for subterranean squeals, watched for the
sudden dart of terrified rabbits, and for the eager inquisitive
emergence of the baffled ferrets. The spades, digging easily
in the sandy earth, discovered the labyrinths and occasionally a nest of newly-born rabbits.

There was a wide watery ditch on the south side of the Cow Pasture, inhabited by frogs, which spawned among the cress and king-cups. Beyond were narrow fields, running parallel with the river, lush and marshy. The river itself ran between banks, for it was liable to flood over. Eastward it ran for about half a mile, till it disappeared under a bridge which carried the road near Peacock's farm—the road of the dream engine. By the bridge was a pool with a projecting pier; this was the sheep-dip, where annually the sheep were given some kind of antiseptic bath.

I remember the oily smell of sheep, sheep-shearing, their ludicrous nakedness when first shorn. Most years there was a pet lamb, a weakling that had to be wrapped in blankets before the kitchen fire, fed from a bottle, and gradually nursed into life. His field would be the Green, and we were his playmates until the inevitable day of parting came. We used to think that the long tails of lambs were bitten off by the shepherd, but actually the animals were gelded by this reputedly safe means. The tails of young colts were cut off with special clippers, and then seared with a red-hot iron. The feet of full grown sheep rot and have to be scraped; maggots burrow into their flesh and pullulate, are gouged out and the sheep anointed. Their wool is infested with nauseous black ticks. Only on the moors, where the sheep are black-faced and agile, with curled horns and quivering nostrils, does this animal acquire any dignity.

The greater part of the Farm was given over to various crops—wheat, oats, barley and rye—and the fields devoted to these spread northwards. Some of them seemed very remote to us. One was sinister, for a large oak-tree grew in the middle of it, and here a man sheltering under it had been struck by lightning and killed. Another field, at the extreme north of our land, had high hedges full of may-blossom; there was a sparse wood on one side; and here, years afterwards when the Farm was only a memory, I staged incidents from the *Morte d'Arthur*.

In the nearer fields we watched the labors of the months. We were aware of the plowing, the harrowing, the roll-ing, the sowing, and finally of the harvest. We followed the plowman, and sometimes ran between the shafts of the plow, pretending to guide it to a truer furrow. At the harvest, as soon as we could walk we became laborers; be-cause then the whole household would turn into the fields, the women to bind the sheaves and pile them into stooks. At lunch-time my Mother would drive out with the buggy laden with sandwiches, cheese and bread, and great stone jars of draught beer. We played at hide-and-seek among the stooks, gathered the shorn poppies and cornflowers, watched the field-mice scurry in fright among the stubble and scarlet pimpernel. At the end of the harvest, the last wagon was escorted back in triumph, often late at night in the moon-light, and a great harvest supper was spread in the kitchen, at which my Father and Mother presided.

In November the hedges were trimmed and layered; the thorns were raked up into great heaps and fired. When we were old enough, my Father would have a cart-load of thorns pitched on the Green, and there one night we would dance round the bonfire.

Almost in the middle of the Farm was the fox-covert—a piece of land of perhaps four acres, thickly covered with gorse and scrub, hedged with hazel trees. Twice in a season the Hunt met at our house. They assembled on the Green —the Master, the Kennelman and several others in their scarlet coats and peaked caps, the farmers and their ladies in hard billy-cock hats. The hounds moved in a compact mass, their upcurved tails swaying rhythmically. When the Meet was present, they moved off to the fox-covert, and always without much difficulty started a fox. My Father rode one of his beautiful hunters; my Mother had her pony. At first we children went on foot as far as the Covert and saw them take off, and piped our tally-ho's if we caught sight of the fox. We heard the huntsman's horn as they sped across the fields, waited until we could hear it no more, then went home to wait until the weary hunters returned. But when I was about seven I was given my first pony, and then rode away with the hounds—my first hunt ending in the middle of a hedge which my impetuous pony had taken too rashly.

At the first kill at which I was present I had to be 'blooded.' The severed head of the fox was wiped across my face till it was completely smeared in blood, and I was told what a fine huntsman I should make. I do not remember the blood, nor the joking huntsmen; only the plumed breath of the horses, the jingle of their harness, the beads of dew and the white gossamer on the tangled hedge beside us.

8

THE ABBEY

OCCASIONALLY we made excursions to regions beyond the Farm. Once a year, perhaps in early Autumn, we went with wagons to some woods eight or nine miles away, on the edge of the moors. There we had the right to fell a certain amount of timber, and to bring it away on our wagons. It was a long day's expedition, and an immense adventure when we were allowed to go. We took our food with us and picnicked among the resinous chips and stripped bark.

This is the only expedition I remember taking from the Farm. My wider explorations were done from other bases. Three or four times, in times of illness or when, I now suppose, a brother or sister was expected, I went to stay with relations for a few weeks. My Mother was the youngest daughter in a family of nine, so we were richly provided with aunts. One of these, a widow, lived with her two sons and our Grandfather in a cottage at Helmsley, and there I stayed on at least two occasions.

Helmsley was six miles to the west. The road passed through Harome, a hamlet of white thatched cottages, in one of which lived a woman, my Mother used to tell us impressively, with twenty-three children. A mile outside Helmsley the road crossed the railway, and then ran in a straight slope into the town. My Aunt's cottage was on the right as we entered, by the side of a saw-mill. When a saw was working a high melancholy whine rose above the houses and filled me with a vague dread. This first street, Bondgate, opened into a wide market-place, with a market-cross and a monument in the middle. On one side the houses were still half timbered, with overhanging gables; the tower of the Church rose above them, scattering a merry peal from its numerous bells. Once a week, on Saturdays, the market-place was filled with booths, dense with farmers and their wives. At other times it was a wide deserted space, with perhaps a child or two and a dog at the foot of the cross. Sometimes a cart drawn by bullocks passed slowly across, as if to emphasize an air of almost Eastern sleepiness—such carts being an affectation of the Earl whose park gates were at the end of one of the streets leading out of the market-place.

Beyond the market-place stood the castle with its ivied keep, still massive and imposing in spite of deliberate destruction by the Parliamentarians. Here again was a stage-setting for my later romantic notions, but my authentic memory of this time only associates it with a tennis tournament in which my Father took part, and I still see the white figures of the players set against the vivid green of the lawn. Sheep grazed in the empty moats and jackdaws nested in the ragged turrets. The castle might have been more impressive but for still more romantic monuments within my reach. Duncombe Park was an amazing wonderland, which we entered but rarely, and always with an awe communicated by our deferential elders. My eyes searched the wide vistas for some limiting hedge, but in vain. We stopped to stroke a newly-born deer. Vanbrugh's mansion was something beyond my comprehension, of which I only preserve, as fragments from a strange feast, the white ghosts of marble statues incongruous in this greenery, an orange-tree in fruit in the conservatory, and a thatched ice-house. Overhanging a steep valley at the end of the park is a famous terrace, with a lawn as smooth as a carpet and a Grecian temple at each end. Down in this valley is the abbey of Rievaulx.

Rievaulx played an important part in the growth of my imagination, but I cannot tell how much of its beauty and romance was absorbed in these years of childhood, how much built on to these memories in later years. It was the farthest western limit of my wanderings, and so lovely then in its solitude and desolation, that I think my childish mind, in spite of its overweening objectivity, must have surrendered to its subtle atmosphere. One day, years later, I happened to be there when a new church, built under the shadow of the ruins, was consecrated. A choir had come from York Minster, and sang a *Te Deum* between the ruined arches; their sweet voices echoing strangely under the roof of the sky, their white surplices fluttering in the wind. The tomb of Sir Walter l'Espec, the knight who had founded the abbey and had afterwards died as a monk in these cloisters, stood at the end of the chancel. It was not dedicated to any known God, but in a moment of solitude it would serve as an altar to a sense of glory denoted by these ruins and this tomb, and their existence in this solitary place.

Around Rievaulx, and especially through the narrow wooded dales which strike like green rays into the purple darkness of the Moors, I wandered with my cousin, a boy five or six years older than myself. He was a keen collector of birds' eggs, butterflies and flowers, and had great cunning in the pursuit of these objects. From him I learned how to handle birds' eggs, to empty them through one blow-hole, to pack them in match-boxes. We carried catapults and I was taught the honor of the chase: which birds it was legitimate to shoot, how many eggs one could take from a nest, how to rob a nest without spoiling it or discouraging the mother-bird. One day in mistake I shot a robin, a crime my cousin made more terrible by promising to keep it a secret from the world.

Sometimes we would be out all day, regardless of meals. We gathered wild gooseberries and stewed them in a tin over a fire of twigs. We ate the tender shoots of sweet-briar, sorrel and pig-nuts. I imagine we were severely scolded on our return, but such unpleasantnesses do not endure in the memory. I remember instead the upright figure of my Grandfather, white-haired and gentle in his armchair by the kitchen fire, the singing kettle and the cheeping cry of the crickets. We had only candles to light the cottage in the evening. There was a long window full of geraniums, a steep wooden staircase with a latched door that clicked loudly. In this house I have always pictured the story of the Three Bears.

Behind it was a long straggling yard, with outhouses belonging to a builder, and at the end a walled garden where my Grandfather grew vegetables and kept bees in straw hives. The privy was here too, and a shed containing, among other junk, some old gas pipes from which I used to try and construct a fountain. I have never met again their pungent metallic smell. Beyond the garden was a lane leading to the cemetery, which with its orderliness and symbolic cypresses was a place very different from the graveyard at Kirkdale. It was usually bright with flowers, and the Sisters of Mercy passed along the graveled paths with their billowing black robes and white-winged caps. I see now that there was something a little foreign in the whole aspect of this town, with its highly ritualistic church, cloudy with sweet incense, where men and women sat in opposite aisles, its tyrannical vicar, its musical bells, its cart-oxen and its air of seeming to live intently on the four sides of a wide open square.

9

THE CHURCH

E VERY Sunday the dog-cart was yoked up and the
whole family climbed into the high seats, my Father
and Mother in front with the youngest of us between them,
the rest of us clinging to the precarious back-seat. When it
rained an immense gingham umbrella, like the roof of a
pagoda, sheltered us all. The big wheels crunched on the
gritty roads. The Farm retreated from us as we trotted down
the northern road to our Parish Church, five miles away.
The road had three points of interest: the Little Beck, the
Big Beck, and the peacocks. The becks excited us because
they had no bridges: they widened out into shallow fords
through which the horse splashed as if born to this watery
element. In Spring the becks were often flooded, and sometimes the water stretched for hundreds of feet in a lake of
incalculable depth. Then the excitement was intense, but
my Father must have known the safe limits of the flood. I
remember the water coming up to the horse's belly, and our
anxiety for the rug, which had a way of hanging below the
footboard.

About a mile before we reached the Church we passed a
small village in the middle of which was a country-house

known as 'The Hall,' and here, on a high wall, we sometimes saw the peacocks which inhabited the garden beyond.
For us they were fabulous birds, and the glory of their
plumage the most exotic sight of those days. A mile farther
on, the road descended steeply into a narrow valley, and
there, in complete isolation, stood our Church. First came
a row of sheds and stables, where the horse was unyoked and
the trap put under shelter. Then the path led a little lower
down to the gate of the churchyard, where in Summer a
few men would be standing, enjoying the air until the last
moment. The bell, or rather the clapper, clanged in the
squat tower. The Church is of gray stone with a slated
roof, and stands out clearly as you approach it against a
dark wood of firs. Ancient tombstones lean out of the
grassy mounds at all angles. We were taught that it was
wicked to walk over a grave, but this graveyard is so ancient
and so thickly populated, that we had to wander as if in a
maze. Either before or after the service we made our way
to the family graves, at the east end of the Church; but it
was not until Mariana died that this duty became a melancholy one, the sight of my Mother's tears communicating a
wondering sense of woe.

In Summer we brought flowers to this grave, and sometimes I was sent to throw away the withered remains of last
week's wreath. At the end of the churchyard there was a
low wall, and below this a deep ravine in which the river
ran, quite overshadowed by trees. Into this gloomy cavern
I threw my handfuls of wisps, glad to hide my uneasiness
in this gesture.

Over the porch of the Church is a famous Saxon sundial

with an inscription carved on the stone panels at each side which tells us that Orm the son of Gamal bought Saint Gregory's minster when it was all broken down and fallen, and he caused it to be made new from the ground, to Christ and Saint Gregory, in the reign of Edward the King, in the days of Tosti the Earl. Round the dial itself are the words:

> THIS IS DÆGES SOL MERCA ÆT
> ILCVMTIDE

—this is the day's sun mark at every tide; and below the dial is written: Hawarth made me and Brand the priest.

Inside, the walls are white-washed, and an aqueous light filters through the foliage-bound windows. The nave was then filled with square box-pews, very high, so that we retired into a little private world, to pray as a family safe from the distractions of less familiar human beings. But the family included our Howkeld relations, of whom I shall soon speak; and my Uncle, so patriarchal in his crisp white beard, officiated within our box. He was too stout to kneel on the hassocks which saved our knees from the cold stone floor, but the rest of us, sometimes eight or nine in number, knelt rigidly with hands pressed palm to palm.

The service was of extreme simplicity and dispatch. The sermon never lasted more than ten minutes, sometimes only five. The music came from a small harmonium, and there was a surpliced choir of perhaps two men and three boys. The congregation numbered in all not more than forty— many less when the weather was wild. In Winter the Church was very cold, so we kept our overcoats on, and our breath issued in plumes as we sang the hymns. Once a month there was a Communion Service, and then for a few minutes, when our elders went to receive the Sacrament, we were left in possession of the box, at liberty to fidget and to let our eyes wander to the heraldic monsters displayed on the painted wooden hatchments, to the gallery where the servants sat, and to the trees waving across the leaded trellis of the windows.

After the service (which alternated each week between morning and afternoon, for the vicar served two parishes) the congregation gathered in groups and chatted peacefully as they walked up the path to the gate, and waited for the traps to be yoked up. The inhuman stillness of the situation aided our friendliness; our Church was still where the monks who first built it twelve centuries ago had wanted it to be, in a wild valley, near a running beck, gray like a wild hawk nesting in a shelter of dark trees.

10

THE MILL

ABOUT half a mile above the Church the beck suddenly slackens; part of its waters (in Summer all) disappear down a fissure in the rocky bed. They keep to a subterranean channel for a mile and a half and suddenly reappear, bubbling up from a great depth, at the head of a field which belonged to my Uncle, whose small estate was on that account called Howkeld, which means 'springhead.' Here we came often and always with great joy, as to an enchanted kingdom. My Uncle was a miller, and the mysterious water, which left its proper course and dived underground as if on very purpose to come up again in this particular spot to offer him its services, ran deep and strong in a willow-fringed bend round the large field separating the mill from the road. At the end of the field it became a walled dam, and to the right overflowed through a sluice into a round lake, which acted as a reservoir for times of drought. The private road to the mill followed the course of the stream and the dam, and then crossed by a bridge under which the water disappeared, combed by an iron grill. It emerged in a swift channel at the other side, and then sluiced in a roaring torrent over the water-wheel. The churned water fell in a dazzling white foaming cascade to a whirling pool below the wheel, and then flowed away with diminishing contortions in a stream which ran round the large gardens and through the fields until it rejoined the mother stream a mile and a half farther south.

There was so much here for childish wonder! The mill itself, with its swinging straps and flickering wheels, the bright chains that hoisted the grain to the top story, the dusty machines in which we could see, through little windows, the grain trickling, and the general earth-shaking hum and whirr. The foreman's bright eyes twinkled from a face all powdered with flour, his clothes were like white mouse-skin, his beard hoary. His voice was piping high, from having to make himself heard in the din. On Sundays, when the mill was still, flour-dust deadened the sound of our feet on the worn wooden floors; our hands ran sweetly along smooth step-ladders and horny ropes.

Perhaps because there was always a plentiful supply of grain, my Aunt kept all kinds of poultry, and in the yard round the mill the most motley assembly of fowls strutted and pecked—not only various breeds of hens, but guinea-fowl, turkeys, ducks and geese. The house was at the end of the yard, T-shaped, its leg in line with the mill. A side door led into the leg, which was a low extension of the original building and here was the Little Room where the family always lived, except on festive occasions. It was a very low room with a varnished wooden beam running across the ceiling. Most of the space was taken up by a sideboard and a large dining-table, and it is hard to think of this room without its complement of food. This was always spread in the most lavish way, with great hams and sirloins of beef, pies, pastries and puddings, and, at tea-time, cakes and tarts of the most alluring kind. My Aunt was a famous cook: the mill and the gardens and the farm poured forth their plenty at the doorstep; by barter, in exchange for flour, most of the other essentials and luxuries of life were forthcoming. A deep spring of purest water flowed in the nearest field. War and famine could pass over the land and leave such bounty unaffected.

It was always peaceful here, a peace of guelder-roses and peonies, of laden fruit-trees and patient waters. Perhaps this impression means that our visits were mainly confined to the Summer; in Winter I only remember the frozen lake, on which we learned to skate. People came from far and near on such occasions, and the ice rang with the swift metallic strokes of the skaters' feet. In Summer the lake, round which a path led among the reeds and rushes, was given over to the water-hens and wild ducks. Sometimes a flight of wild geese would come sweeping out of the sky on their way north.

I have already described my Uncle as patriarchal, and this was true of him in more than appearance. My Aunt was the eldest (and my Mother the youngest) of the large family I have already mentioned. Some of these had married and migrated to other parts of the world, but such as remained, a goodly number, looked up to my Uncle as the head of the clan into which he had married. His stout figure, his crisp white beard and twinkling eyes, his little linen bags of sample grain, his chuckle and his soft rich dialect, were familiar to the whole countryside; and at the time I speak of he was blessed with much happiness and prosperity. But during the next thirty years (he lived to be nearly ninety) he was to suffer many afflictions: the death of his favorite son, the bankruptcy of another, followed by the mortgaging of his own estate and finally a moratorium—and during all these tribulations he remained, a Lear of these Steppes, magnificent in courage and faith.

His children were contemporaries of my Father and Mother, and this introduced complications into our childish minds, for we called our cousins simply by their Christian names, whilst others who seemed their equals were aunts and uncles. The youngest of these cousins was not too old to despise the part of guide and initiator. One day he organized an expedition to explore the cave at Kirkdale. This famous cave extends for three hundred feet underground, and has more than one branch inside. The expedition, therefore, had to be undertaken with proper precautions. These consisted of candles, a large ball of binder-band, and the retriever, Jet. At the entry of the cave we made the end of the band secure, lit our candles, and crept forward unrolling the ball as we went. The sides of the cave glistened in the candle-light; drops of moisture fell from the stalactites above us; the air we breathed was cold and dank. I cannot remember how far we penetrated, but at one point we were terrified by the sudden appearance of two fiery eyes in the darkness confronting us. Could it be one of the ancient hyenas, not yet a remnant of bones? But it was only Jet, who had run round some loop in the cave and come to meet us.

Once or twice we made expeditions up the dale beyond the cave and the Church. It is one of the wildest and most

beautiful places in the whole country; and I still remember
my Father driving some fine lady from the outer world
along the track which went along the ridge of the dale, and
how she swore that it was more beautiful than Switzerland,
a country of which we had no conception, but which we
thought must be wonderful because people traveled far just
to look at its hills and dales. This track up the dale ended at
a house about two miles from the Church; here the dale became narrower and was filled with thick woods where lilies
grew. No road led through these woods, not even a path;
but an adventurous spirit could make his way along the bed
of the stream, and after a mile or two he would discover that
the dale opened out again, to give space to a mill and a few
farms and cottages. This is Bransdale, an oasis on the Moors,
which in our time only had a poor moorland track to link it
with the outer world. The people who lived here were
strange and dark and beautiful, even to my childish eyes.
For sometimes, when staying at Howkeld, I would go out
for the day with the wagoners. Our load of grain and flour
was drawn by great shaggy-footed cart-horses, their harness
bright with brass ornaments, their manes and tails plaited
with colored ribbons—drawn over the wide purple Moors,
where God seems to have left the earth clear of feature to
reveal the beauty of its naked form, till we dipped down into
the green dales and lifted our burden.

THE ATTIC

THE successive governesses who helped my Mother with our upbringing remain utterly vague to me. They must have occupied a large place in our lives, but except for one insubstantial ghost of dark hair and spectacles, none of them can I recall. I know that they taught us to read, but I doubt if I had acquired that accomplishment before the age of seven. Then books immediately became my element. There was nothing to encourage me in this taste: there were no books in the living-rooms, and my Father read little except the *Yorkshire Post* and various agricultural papers. On Sunday he would read to us the lessons of the day (perhaps this was only when it was impossible to go to Kirkdale) and he made us learn the Collect by heart. The only book of his I still possess is *The Poetical Works of Sir Walter Scott*. My Mother read to us often, especially *Little Arthur's History of England, Evenings at Home, Forget-me-not,* and a tendentious story published by the Religious Tract Society called *Little Meg's Children* (by the author of *Jessica's First Prayer, the Children of Cloverley,* etc.). I still possess *Little Meg's Children,* and I see now that its grim pathos, too simple to be wholly sentimental, may have worked into the tex-

46

ture of my unfolding imagination, above all to prepare me for the shock of death which waited for me so near; for the first chapter describes the death of Little Meg's mother, and the plight of the orphaned children. The book as a whole might not survive any critical inspection; but am I still bound to childish wonder when I feel some merit in sentences like these?

'She turned her face round to the wall with a deep sigh, and closed her eyelids, but her lips kept moving silently from time to time. Meg cried softly to herself in her chair before the fire, but presently she dozed a little for very heaviness of heart, and dreamed that her father's ship was come into dock, and she, and her mother, and the children, were going down the dingy streets to meet him. She awoke with a start; and creeping gently to her mother's side, laid her warm little hand upon hers. It was deadly cold with a chill such as little Meg had never before felt; and when her mother neither moved nor spoke in answer to her repeated cries, she knew that she was dead.

'For the next day, and the night following, the corpse of the mother lay silent and motionless in the room where her three children were living. Meg cried bitterly at first; but there was Robin to be comforted, and the baby to be played with when it laughed and crowed in her face. Robin was nearly six years old, and had gained a vague dim knowledge of death, by having followed, with a troop of other curious children, many a funeral that had gone out from the dense and dirty dwellings to the distant cemetery, where he had crept forward to the edge of the grave, and peeped down into what seemed to him a very dark and dreadful depth.

When little Meg told him mother was dead, and lifted him up to kneel on the bedside, and kiss her icy lips for the last time, his childish heart was filled with an awe which almost made him shrink from the sight of that familiar face, scarcely whiter or more sunken now than it had been for many a day past. . . .'

We must have wept often over the tribulations of Little Meg, and may have been duly impressed by her Christian constancy. Were we held by anything but the pathos of the story? This strange country of dingy streets and attics (an attic perhaps I could visualize), of lack of bread and clothes, of evil and misery—it was as fairy-like as any story that I had heard—as hard to realize, but just as easy to believe. The emotions were involved, and the imagination, but nothing like reflection or reasoning. We were moved in exactly the same way, and perhaps even to a greater degree, by the adventures of Little Red Ridinghood. Both she and Meg were 'Little,' and both survived the perils they encountered. When even the perils we ourselves encounter as children leave so little impression on our sensibility (just because we have no reasoning power to trace their consequences) why should the fictitious pathos of a story have more effect? The perturbations of the intellect are a danger to the instinctive basis of life; no wonder, then, that nature is wise enough to wrap us in a cocoon of insensibility, until such time as we have the power to counter intelligence with deeper intuitions.

Little Meg's attic could be visualized because we had our own attic at the top of the house. It was approached by a steep staircase just outside the nursery door. On the left, when you reached the top, were two bedrooms, partitioned off and occupied by the maids. But the rest of the space under the roof was free. One side was used for storing apples, and their musty sweetness pervaded the whole room. There were several chests and wardrobes, full of old wedding-dresses, and many other things which I do not distinctly remember. But here also was the only considerable store of books in the house, a miscellaneous collection of foxed volumes of sermons and devotional works which can have had little appeal to me, but which I pored over with an instinctive love. But two larger tomes were an inexhaustible mine of delight. They were bound volumes of the *Illustrated London News* for the year of the Great Exhibition (presumably 1850), full of the steel engravings of the period.

My lust for books was not satisfied in the attic; I soon craved for novelty. But I must have realized thus early that such a longing was a personal affair, to be fulfilled only by a personal effort. Looking round for a means to this end, I seized on the postman as the only link with the printed world. He came daily on his long pedestrian round, for if there were no letters to bring, there was always the *Yorkshire Post*. I made friends with him, and confided to him my secret desires. He was sympathetic, but his acquaintance with literature was limited. It was limited, in fact, to a lurid pink periodical called, I think, *The Police Gazette,* and this he passed on to me; but though I remember the act of reading it, it left no particular impression on me. Evidently its contents had none of the reality of a fairy world.

I return again and again, in retrospection, to this early untutored interest in books, for how could it have developed, in such isolation and such neglect, but for the presence of some inborn disposition. And faith in such a disposition becomes, with the growth of the personality, a controlling factor. At least, we are only happy so long as our life expands in ever widening circles from the upward gush of our early impulses; and even love, of which the child is ignorant, is only real in so far as it is a transformation, in adolescence, of our first instinctive attachments.

12

THE MUSICAL BOX

ONE day my Father brought a delightful toy back from Northallerton: it was a small musical box which played 'For there's nae luck about the house.' But my Mother, perhaps then, or perhaps shortly afterwards, when there was sufficient cause, thought the tune was ominous. My only sister was a baby then, between two and three years old. Our Farm was called the Grange, and though it had no moat, this daughter was christened Mariana. Perhaps that too was ominous, for a sad song goes by her name. Mariana was fair as sunlight, and smiled to the tinkle of the musical box. And that is all I remember of her, for that Spring I was suddenly sent away. A few days later my Aunt told me that Mariana had become an angel, and the next time we went to Kirkdale I was taken to see the unmeaning mound that covered her body.

Apart from this fatal musical box, the only other music I ever heard in my childhood was Fiddler Dick's. Every year the young horses bred on the Farm had to be 'broken in,' and this was work for a specialist, who, like the blacksmith, paid us periodical visits. Fiddler Dick was a natty little man, with a hot swarthy complexion and waxed mustaches—

probably he was of gypsy blood. He would stay a few days at the Farm, sleeping in the loft above the saddle-room. He always brought his fiddle with him, and after dinner, or in the evening, used to play to a wondering audience. I was fascinated by this man—fascinated when he stood in the Cow Pasture, his neat leggings winking in the sunshine, a wild young colt galloping, trotting, walking in a circle at the end of a long rope, controlled by Fiddler Dick's flicking whip—still more fascinated when the brown fiddle came out of its box and a sound, never imagined before, was conjured out of the air. Now, I had seen, in a chest in the attic, just such a brown fiddle, and one day when Fiddler Dick was at the Farm, I brought it down and asked him to teach me to make such music. But some of the strings were broken, and the bow had no horse-hair. Some untwisted binder-band served to repair the bow, and we got some cat-gut from the nearest cobbler for the strings. Fiddler Dick rejoiced in the word cat-gut, and cats took on a new significance for me. I cannot now believe that the sounds which issued from this improvised instrument bore any resemblance to the plaintive voice of a violin, but I retained my longing to play. Later, when I went away to school, I persuaded my Mother to let me take music as an extra subject, and she consented. But I was put to the piano, which had no charm for me, no urgency of aspiration. I could not rival Fiddler Dick on such an instrument! Besides, instead of Fiddler Dick, I had for a teacher a fierce Dutchman, bristling with long hair and a silk bow-tie, flashing with rings. At the end of the year my enthusiasm had so waned that I could not urge my Mother to pay the extra fees for music. But I still clung to the old violin, with the vague hope that I might one day learn to play it. It was still in my possession at the beginning of the War, but my Mother died at this time, and in the subsequent confusion the violin disappeared. I had expected to find it among the few possessions I had stored in a cellar against my return, but it was not there. I should perhaps never have given it another thought but for an experience of several years later. I came late one evening, after a walk along a forest road in Bavaria, the moon staring at me through the cage-bars of the trees, to a large castle where many guests were being entertained. Supper was finished and there was not a soul to be seen, except a porter who took my bag, and told me that everyone was in the music-room—even the servants—and that I had better make my way there and wait for the end. I was directed to a small balcony, which I could enter without disturbing the audience. The room was in darkness, except for an electric lamp at the far end of the room, above the dais where the music was being played. It was a violin sonata, and I was immediately held, not so much by the music as by the image which came into my mind as I gazed at the woman playing the violin. Her slender body was like a stem on which nodded, to the rhythm of the music, a strange exotic flower. The corolla of this flower was a human face, very white beneath an arch of raven black hair, and it seemed to brood over the coiled tawny petals of the instrument, preserving an essential stillness in the midst of the force that agitated them. The notes of the piano, to whose rise and fall it seemed bound in some inevitable way, might have been the voice of a stream urging its way past the resisting stem of the flower which swayed above its swift current.

All my early fascination for this instrument, awakened long before by Fiddler Dick and long dormant, awoke again at this moment with a glow in which there was no longer any sense of aspiration or self-directed interest, a fire of renunciation and surrender. Once more an early impulse had found its fulfilment, its transformation, to become a conscious interest in my life.

13

DEATH

THESE scenes of childhood end abruptly with the death of my Father. In the Winter of my ninth year, he was taken ill with pneumonia; and the house became muted and silent. Mrs. Walker, the nurse from one of the cottages by Peacock's farm, whom I have not mentioned before, but who had attended my Mother in all her confinements, was called in; and our cousin the Doctor came from Kirby daily. He and my Father were fast friends, and when the illness became critical, all his energies were devoted to the saving of this precious life. But in vain. Rheumatic fever developed. The air of anguish in everyone, my Mother's tearful eyes—these were obvious even to us children. One day leeches were brought, and stood in a glass jar on a shelf in the dairy. They were black, blind and sinister. But then we were taken away. I went to Howkeld, and one night I suffered intolerable earache, so that I cried aloud, and was poulticed with onions. The pain had gone in the morning, but by my Aunt's tears I knew that my Father was dead. The next day I was driven back to the farm. The blinds were drawn, everywhere it was very still, and dark. We were taken upstairs to say good-bye to my dead Father. The cold wintry light came evenly through the open slats of the venetian blind. My Father lay on the bed, sleeping, as he always did, with his arms on the coverlet, straight down each side of his body. His beautiful face was very white, except for the red marks on his temples, where the leeches had clung. I was told to kiss that face; it was deadly cold, like the face of Little Meg's mother.

I felt stunned, but could not comprehend my loss, nor the grief of those about me. I moved away in the unnatural stillness, walking in a living sleep. Downstairs candles were burning on a table laden with cold meat and cakes. Then we all drove to Kirkdale, slowly over the frozen flint roads, and there a grave was ready dug at the east end of the Church, by the side of Mariana's. The dark cirque of fir-trees rose in the background, sighing in the frosty wind. The bell in the gray tower clanged its toneless note. The horses were not unyoked. Six friends of my Father carried his coffin into the ancient Church, and then to the grave. The earth fell with a hollow sound on to the lowered coffin. My Mother sobbed against my Uncle's shoulder. The last Amen was murmured in that immemorial stillness, and when we had taken a last look at the forlorn coffin, we drove back swiftly over the frozen flint roads, horse-hooves beating clearly in the metallic air.

A few weeks later the sheep were driven into pens, the cattle labeled, and a crowd of farmers from far and near assembled at the Farm. A wagon was drawn out on the Green, to serve as a platform for the auctioneer. Everything was sold, except a few pieces of old furniture which my

Mother was fond of—even the books from the attic, the sermons tied in bundles, and the two volumes of the *Illustrated London News. Little Meg, Little Arthur, Evenings at Home,* and *Forget-me-not* alone were left for me.

We went to stay with a cousin at the other end of the Vale, but only for a few months. Then my eldest brother and I left for a boarding-school, far away from these scenes; my childhood, the first phase of my life, was isolated: it grew detached in my memory and floated away like a leaf on a stream. But it never finally disappeared, as these pages witness. Instead, as this body of mine passes through the rays of experience, it meets bright points of ecstasy which come from the heart of this lost realm. But the realm is never wholly lost: it is reconstructed stage by stage whenever the sensibility recovers its first innocence, whenever eye and ear and touch and tongue and quivering nostril revive sensation in all its child-godly passivity.

Today I found a withered stem of honesty, and shelled the pods between my thumb and finger; silver pennies, which grew between the fragrant currant-bushes. Their glistening surfaces, seeded, the very faint rustle they make in the wind—these sensations come direct to me from a moment thirty years ago. As they expand in my mind, they carry everything in their widening circle—the low crisp box-hedge which would be at my feet, the pear trees on the wall behind me, the potato-flowers on the patch beyond the bushes, the ivy-clad privy at the end of the path, the cow pasture, the fairy rings—everything shimmers for a second on the expanding rim of my memory. The farthest tremor of this perturbation is lost only at the finest edge where sensation passes beyond the confines of experience; for memory is a flower which only opens fully in the kingdom of Heaven, where the eye is eternally innocent.

PART II

THE FALCON
AND THE DOVE

I

This high-caught hooded Reason broods upon my wrist,
Fettered by a so tenuous leash of steel.
We are bound for the myrtle marshes, many leagues away,
And have a fair expectation of quarry.

II

Over the laggard dove, inclining to green boscage,
Hovers this intentional doom—till the unsullied sky receives
A precipitation of shed feathers
And the swifter fall of wounded wings.

III

Will the plain aye echo with that loud Hullallo!
Or retain an impress of our passage?
We have caught beauty in a wild foray
And now the falcon is hooded and comforted away.

A CALLOW NESTLING

IT WILL have been seen that there was nothing very exceptional in the circumstances of my childhood: it was the childhood of any farmer's son in the remote English countryside of that time. If it now seems to belong to another world, it is because in the past forty years two inventions have transformed that kind of life. The farms have lost their isolation, both in the physical and spiritual sense. I imagine that the modern farmer's boy grows up to the tune of a London dance-band, while across his innocent eye flickers the vision of life offered by Hollywood. He may not be any the worse for it: he would certainly consider my placid environment a poor substitute for his Babylonian excitements. If I would still prefer my kind of childhood, it is because I am introducing into the comparison an adult sense of values. The seclusion of my first ten years now seems like an age of unearthly bliss, a ring in a rock to which all the strands of my subsequent happiness are tied.

One day in the year 1904, a bewildered and fatherless boy, I was quietly withdrawn from this world and taken a devious train journey across the county. I still retain some memory of the nightmarish impression made by the cavernous stations where we changed trains; and I remember our cab rattling along the roughly cobbled streets of the town which was our destination. We climbed up steep hills, past dark satanic mills, and emerged eventually on a high bare moor, at the other side of which rose the largest building I had ever seen. Built of local stone in a style that must, I now realize, have been copied from some monument of the French Renaissance, blackened by the smoke which drifted across the moor from the surrounding factories, this was the orphanage school in which I was to spend the next five years of my life, in an isolation no less absolute than that of my infancy. For six weeks in summer and for a fortnight at Christmas I returned to the countryside, but these were idyllic interludes in what was otherwise a monastic existence. The school, with several acres of ground, was enclosed by high stone walls, and we only passed through these walls, once a week, to march in military formation to a chapel in the town.

I do not intend to write much about this period of my life because I do not think it is of general interest. From the age of ten or eleven to the age of fifteen or sixteen is the least genial period in the life of a boy. He has lost the innocent eye of childhood and has not yet become an experiencing nature. It is a callow and confused phase, in which the mind is unconsciously acquiring its social armor of habits and inhibitions. It is the stage at which the sensibility of most children is irretrievably destroyed. The sense of sin or guilt is imposed on the innocent impulses, and actions lose their animal playfulness. Relations with other people become conscious instead of instinctive: the child has to begin to plot its way through a maze of regulated paths. How it can come through this intricate process with an undimmed vision or any trace of its original freshness is still unknown: but at least we are now aware that we are involved in an educational dilemma. Any too conscious approach to the problem seems fatal, and the best minds and sensibilities are still apt to be the chance products of a casual upbringing.

There were about two hundred boys in the school; in the same building, but strictly segregated, and only visible at meal-times, were about a hundred girls. The regimen was Spartan: no hot water for washing at any time of the year; meat and vegetables once a day and otherwise only milk and bread, mostly dry bread. The discipline was strict, though not tyrannical, and strongly religious in tone. There were no amenities—no private rooms, not even a reading-room. A boy who wished to read a book outside class-hours had to read it in the shrill pandemonium of the common playroom—an exercise to which I attribute my unusual ease of concentration. There were no luxuries; pocket money was forbidden, and though there was a certain amount of secret trading, it had usually exhausted itself by the end of the second or third week of the term. All the menial duties were done by the boys themselves; we made our own beds and cleaned our own boots. We wore a uniform which consisted of gray trousers and waistcoat, an Eton jacket of blue face-cloth, and a pork-pie cap with a straight flat peak of shiny black leather. In winter we walked out in gray Inverness capes.

This monastic establishment has changed out of all recognition since my time: it has been brought into the general line of secondary schools, thrown open to day-boys, and generally modernized. But when I was there, it still maintained all the features of a much earlier conception of education, such as we can find described in the novels of Dickens; it was not essentially different from the Christ's Hospital described by Leigh Hunt in his *Autobiography*. For the first year I had the company of my younger brother; and our third brother joined us in the second year. But I have never lived under such a cloud of unhappiness as fell upon me once we had taken such a brave farewell of our mother and the guardian uncle who had accompanied us on this first journey. I was by disposition of a quiet nature, but no wild animal from the pampas imprisoned in a cage could have felt so hopelessly thwarted. From fields and hedges and the wide open spaces of the moors; from the natural companionship of animals and all the mutations of farm life, I had passed into a confined world of stone walls, smoky skies, and two hundred unknown and apparently unsympathetic strangers. It is true that among the crowd we soon learned to distinguish a group of a dozen or twenty in the same predicament—the 'new boys' or 'newkers' who had arrived on the same day. And each of us was allotted a 'guardian'—an older boy whose duty was to initiate us into the ways of the school. But nothing could relieve the overwhelming desolation of our life, and this state of anguish continued for at least twelve months.

It is not easy for an adult to recollect the quality of his preadolescent emotions. They have been obliterated by thousands of other emotions, which while not necessarily so acute, are more memorable. The emotions of a boy or girl have a baffled intensity which is due to our inability, at that age, to express ourselves. We have found words to describe outward objects, and to express simple sensations, like physical pain. But the vague emotions which are aroused by our environment, by strange experiences, by the unknown—for these we have no ready words. We cannot impart our moods, even to our most intimate friends. Children of this intermediate age suffer like animals, dumbly and vaguely; and the only release is tears. But tears are forbidden by the schoolboy's code, so even that outlet is dammed.

The cure, of course, is action, and perhaps that is why sport is forced on the English schoolboy: it is an example of our instinctive social wisdom. Unfortunately sport is competitive, and if you have neither the physique nor the skill to ensure proficiency, it soon becomes hateful. I was neither good nor bad: merely 'middling,' as we said, and indifference was my general attitude. I played when it was necessary to play; I avoided play when I could. For I had already discovered the joy of reading—had, indeed, brought it with me to school. This predilection I believe to have been innate. I have already, in 'The Innocent Eye,' given evidence of its still earlier manifestations, and I try now, as I tried then, to recollect any influence in my boyhood which might have encouraged this latent tendency. There is none. This taste was self-evident, and I persisted in it against all sorts of obstacles. There was a small miscellaneous library in the school, but it had few volumes to attract a boy of my age. I had no money to buy books: I relied on a small patrimony of my own, and a sporadic system of exchange with other boys. We were, most of us, omnivorous; we read Scott and

Ballantyne, Mayne Reid and Henty, but my own imagination was most strongly fired by Rider Haggard, and never have I known such absorption and excitement as gripped me when I first read *King Solomon's Mines* and *Montezuma's Daughter*.

Such an innate taste for reading, which is merely the vicarious exercise of the imagination, is fairly common among boys; what I next discovered in myself, though I did not at that time attach any significance to it, was a taste for writing. I can trace its first appearance back to the age of thirteen, when I was in the Fifth Form; for three or four of us then produced a surreptitious magazine for which I wrote the serial. By that time this faculty was also leading to more practical results, for the essay, which from now onwards became an important subject, became my best subject, and the only one in which I displayed any exceptional talent. By the time I had reached the Sixth Form, and during the two years I spent there (my fourteenth and fifteenth years) I was taking a very conscious pleasure in this accomplishment. Naturally I was encouraged by some of the masters; I have a vague recollection of representing the school in a national competition; and to these masters, particularly to the headmaster Mr. Barber, who was a man of noble character and fine discrimination, I owe my first perception of literary form and structure. But I insist that the impulse to write, the love of words for their own sake and for the sake of what they could express, was precedent, and no more to be explained by personal influences than the color of my hair or the pitch of my voice.

At the end of our fifteenth year the school cast us, willy-nilly, out into the world. It is an age at which ambitions are scarcely formulated, or are merely fanciful. It is not an age at which a normal boy can make any effective protest against plans made for him by his elders. By this time my mother had left the country to take a post in Leeds, and it was in this city that I was to spend the next six years of my life. I was persuaded to apply for a clerkship in the local Savings Bank. I succeeded in obtaining it; my salary was £20 a year.

The Bank was a venerable institution, with a Head Office in the center of the city and three branches in outlying working-class districts. The junior clerks circulated, month by month, between these four offices. We assembled at the Head Office every morning, where we met the branch manager and picked up the cash-bag. At the branch office we opened the doors at ten o'clock and sat at a desk behind a counter. When a 'depositor' entered, we took his pass-book and money, handed the money to the manager to count, and then entered the amount in the pass-book and in the day-book which we kept on the desk. If the 'depositor' wished to withdraw a sum, we took his pass-book and checked it against the ledger. We closed the doors at three, counted the day's deposits and withdrawals, balanced the day-book, and then made as quickly as possible for the Head Office, carrying the heavy cash-bag. We were free by half-past three or four.

This left a considerable part of the day for further activities. From the beginning I considered the Bank as a stopgap: it did not enter at all into my plan of life. I was under a contract to serve for three years, but this suited me very nicely, for I should then be eighteen or nineteen, the proper age for entering a university. That, at any rate, was an essential stage in life, whatever direction my ambitions might afterwards take. My father's only brother had gone to Cambridge, and my father had always intended that at least one of his sons should follow this example, even if he then returned to the farm. There must often have been talk about this plan in our family circle, and I cannot explain in any other way my early resolution to continue my education. I was not driven to it by my mother or my guardians—indeed, they urged me to make the most of 'the good opening' I had already found; it was my own sense of the necessary future.

Evening schools and the public library provided me with the means of continuing my education, and my time was divided between the Bank and these useful institutions. In my gray cloak and bowler hat I sped through the sooty streets, timid and introspective, and gradually my vague ambitions began to take definite shape. My first idea was to become a doctor. My father's best friend had been a doctor, and perhaps he had become in some degree a father-substitute whom I unconsciously desired to imitate. I began, therefore, to study the sciences, and to collect the prospectuses of various medical schools. But about this time I spent a few weeks recuperating from an illness with this same doctor-friend, and when I confided to him my ambition, he became very distressed, and argued forcibly against my decision. I forget what arguments he used: most likely he was simply convinced that I did not possess the right temperament. In any case, he succeeded in unsettling me, and I began to reconsider the possibilities.

Meanwhile another ferment had arisen almost spontane-ously in my mind—I had become aware of politics. It was probably difficult to avoid them in those days. The great issues of Free Trade and Protection, Home Rule for Ireland, the Disestablishment of the Church, and the Reform of the House of Lords, were being debated with fervor in every newspaper and at every street-corner. Open-air meetings and demonstrations were frequent, and feeling ran high. It became necessary, merely in my daily contacts with my col-leagues in the Bank, to declare some kind of attitude. I did not hesitate: I instinctively adopted the attitude which would have been my father's—I became a true-blue Tory. I eagerly acquired the party propaganda; I read Disraeli's novels and, carried on by my growing intellectual curiosity, grappled with Canning, Burke and Bolingbroke. I joined the local branch of the Conservative Party and distributed leaflets from house to house. I worshiped my King with a blind emotional devotion, and even managed to make a hero out of Lord Salisbury.

This access of political enthusiasm was not without its influence on the trend of my ambitions. I do not think that I ever formulated the idea of a political career with any pre-cision, but I decided to exchange medicine for law. When I announced this decision, my mother and her advisers were well pleased, and immediately began to devise ways and means of articling me to a solicitor. But this prospect was not altogether agreeable to me. I already realized that the difference between the two branches of the legal profession was the difference between drab realism and romantic potentialities, and I was determined to be a barrister. The difficulties, especially the financial ones, were pointed out to me, and they seemed insurmountable. I weakened to the extent of allowing negotiations with a solicitor to begin; but meanwhile my evening studies had been progressing and I had sat for the matriculation examination. It was in the midst of these negotiations that I passed this Rubicon, and this preliminary success gave me the necessary self-confidence and resolution. I announced my determination to proceed to the University, and to let the question of a career depend on what happened to me there. The problem of financing my studies still remained to be settled, but I had a plan. My grandfather, who had died while I was still at school, had left me a legacy of £300 which was not to become due until I attained the age of twenty-five. I went to an uncle of my father's, a sheep-farmer who was reputed to be rich, and asked him to lend me the necessary money for fees and board on the security of this legacy. He was a dour and silent man, but he had no boys of his own and I think I touched his heart. He consented and the way was open.

This narrative has become much more trivial and personal than I at first intended. There is nothing very unusual in the events I have related, but they do lead to a crisis in my life, and the resolution of that crisis was an act of my own will, carried out in face of general disapproval and even the active opposition of some of my relatives. Such a crisis comes in the lives of most poor but ambitious youths, and it is of some general interest to try and determine the decisive factors. The alignment of forces is always the same: on the one side the caution of parents and guardians, anxious to guide the youth towards some position of economic security and immediate yield; on the other side the youth's self-projection into the future, the fantasy which he has formed of his life, his will to power. If there is no question of immediate or proximate need—if money is no object, as we say—then the crisis is not very intense. It is argued in social terms. To many it will be merely a question of traditional behavior: the particular public school and the particular college in the University are as predetermined as the cut of the clothes or the accent of speech. The question whether the son of a rich manufacturer should go to Oxford or not (I ignore the finer problem of Oxford or Cambridge) is largely a question of whether the personal contacts he is likely to make there will raise the social status of the family, be good for business, and even lead to a good marriage. To another large class it is a question of a necessary routine: the boy who is destined to be a teacher, a doctor, a technician or a scientist, must go through the mill and acquire the necessary qualifications. Ambition in such cases is specific and narrow, practical rather than romantic. It astonished me to find when I first entered the University of Leeds that the ambitions of ninety out of every hundred of my fellow undergraduates were crude and calculating. They were interested in one thing only—in getting the best possible degree by the shortest possible method. They were anxious to memorize and eager to anticipate the testing questions. Their career was plotted and they were careful not to stray from the thin line which marked an easy path through the world of knowledge. Perhaps they had been caught young, in a machine which hitherto I had accidentally escaped: they had been selected, in the various centers of popular education from which they came, as 'likely winners.' The scholarships which they had won had already lifted them out of the class into which they had been born—had saved them from the mine or the mill; and they were content with their prescribed destiny. A few of them would, during their three or four years at the university, betray still more exceptional virtues, and this élite would be held back for research scholarships and academic honors; for a machine must have its attendants.

Why should the quality of my ambitions have been so relatively vague and indeterminate? It was partly my ignorance of the realities: I simply did not know the ropes of the educational ladder, and had formed a desperate expedient of wings. I would fly to the heights that I could not scale pedestrianly, sustained by my active imagination. This faculty, which had grown unchecked in infancy, which had not been through the mold of a normal education, which had had time to expand whilst I wandered like a solitary little alien in the streets of Leeds, now knew no limits. It threw into the cloudy future an infinite ray in which there could always be seen, like a silver knight on a white steed, this unreal figure which was myself, riding to quixotic combats, attaining a blinding and indefinable glory.

2

THE DISCOVERY OF
POETRY

IT WAS not until my seventeenth year that I became conscious of the art of poetry. At school we read and even acted Shakespeare, and there were 'recitations' which must have included some verse. But I never read a volume of poems for choice. It was only later, when I began to read for my matriculation, that I also began to listen more intently to the sound of what I was reading: words and phrases would now linger insistently in my mind. At the evening school I attended there was a teacher who had a genuine enthusiasm for his subject; he read aloud to us with feeling and expressiveness. He communicated his pleasure in poetry to at least one of his pupils. About the same time I made the acquaintance of one who was for many years to be my only confidant and my devoted patron. My brother, eighteen months younger than myself, had left school and found employment with a tailor in the city, who bore our family name—even the same Christian name as my brother—and childless himself, henceforth was to take a great interest in all of us. He belonged to a good Quaker family settled for many generations in the Isle of Axholme. Orphaned at an early age, he had been given into the care of two rich and cultured maiden aunts, who gave him a good education and destined him for a post in the British Museum. But at the age of sixteen or so he had suddenly revolted against the smug religious atmosphere in which he was being brought up, and he had run away. After various adventures he had been compelled to take whatever employment he could get, and this happened to be tailoring, a craft for which he had no liking, but which he was to follow for more than forty years with a quiet stoicism. He was a man of small proportions, gentle manners, and in physiognomy bore a close resemblance to the portraits of William Blake. He had two passions—the reading of poetry and the cultivation of flowers. His reading in every direction was wide, and it was in his house that I first made the acquaintance, not only of innumerable volumes of verse, but of the works of writers like Ibsen, Turgenev, Dostoevsky and Chekhov.

Hitherto my reading had been confined to what could be borrowed from the public library, and what I could buy out of an allowance of one shilling a week which I made to myself out of my meager earnings as a bank-clerk. But now I not only had an enthusiast's library to draw from, but I rarely visited this friend without coming away with a gift of two or three volumes. It was probably to my advantage then that the blessings thus showered on me were indiscriminate. My friend praised with equal zest W. B. Yeats and Fiona Macleod, Browning and William Cullen Bryant,

Francis Thompson and Sir Edwin Arnold. If I failed to share his enthusiasm—as in the case of Emerson—he did not question or complain: he was convinced that I should one day see the light.

I cannot now be certain whether my own first poems preceded this fruitful friendship: I think they did. But I cannot forget the emotion with which my mentor learned for the first time that I was writing verses, and with what eagerness he received my efforts when I offered them for his criticism. His criticism was not very severe, though it did check my absurdities. But for the most part he encouraged me with his praise and was for a long time the only audience I had, but a sufficing one. It is to his memory that I have dedicated my collected poems.

It is difficult to recapture the first access of composition. It descended on me like a frenzy, and a day was not perfect unless it gave birth to a poem. Of one thing I am certain: the breath that first fanned my smoldering tinder was Tennyson's. I soon outgrew Tennyson, and for many years affected to despise him—it was a natural reaction, for we tend to turn on all our adolescent enthusiasms. Now that I have balanced my reactions, and can judge Tennyson with a detached mind, I find that I admire him for qualities which must have appealed, however unconsciously, to my awakening sensibility: for the ease and simplicity of his diction, for a broad if not a very profound intelligence, and for an exact rendering of a special landscape—the watery fens and long dim wolds which were not so remote from my own dales and moors. At times he seems to describe the actual scenes of my own childhood:

THE FALCON AND THE DOVE

The seven elms, the poplars four,
That stand beside my father's door,
........the brook that loves
To purl o'er matted cress and ribbed sand,
Or dimple in the dark of rushy coves,
Drawing into his narrow earthen urn,
In every elbow and turn,
The filter'd tribute of the rough woodland.

There would be more to say in adequate appreciation of this poet—more to discover, perhaps, of poetic merit than we generally admit; and a very curious personality to analyze. But now I only seek to relate my own sensibility to his, and to explain why he in particular should have been the reagent in the first poems precipitated from my mind. It would have been much more normal if my enthusiasm at this time had been for Shelley: but the very abstractness of Shelley's poetry kept him at a distance. Shelley, I would now say, demands a degree of intellectual development which I had not reached by the age of seventeen or eighteen. Tennyson had a more objective appeal and was therefore more open to my simple sensibility.

Even so, there were limits to my powers of absorption, and neither then, nor since, could I read the *Idylls of the King*. Romantic as I was, and am, this particular brand of archaicism has always been repugnant to me. I hate every kind of literary fustian, every affectation of an earlier style, every exercise or experiment in an old measure. Such a whimsy attitude to the art of writing is impossible to anyone who believes in the immediacy of expression, in the automatism of inspiration, in the creative nature of even poetic evolution: and these are the doctrines of a true romanticism. The rest is dilettantism: not the vital function, but an academic diversion.

The compositions which came to me so easily in these adolescent days were destroyed long ago, and I have no very precise recollection of their nature. They were, I think, mostly short lyrics about flowers, birds, atmospheric moods; the more realistic of them may have attempted to catch something of the poetry of foggy, gas-lit streets, the glow of furnaces by night, the clatter of clogs on the stone pavements. There were no love poems, for my heart was not yet engaged.

It was then that the poetry of William Blake descended on me like an apocalypse. Tennyson had chimed in with my moods, and shown me felicity. Blake shook me to the depths of my awakening mind, scattered the world of my objective vision, and left me floundering in subjective fantasy. I did not, at that time, venture far into the Prophetic Books; but the Songs of Innocence and Experience, and the poems from the Rossetti and Pickering manuscripts, pierced me like gleaming steel, and their meaning was annealed to my mind. Their meaning?—I should rather say their mystery, for many of these poems were not easy to understand, and indeed I did not seek to understand them. From the beginning I was content with the incantation of a poem, and I still maintain that this is the quality essential to poetry.

Blake kept his ascendancy in my mind for many years—indeed, though I have submitted to many influences and have been fired to more than one enthusiasm in the intervening years, there is no poet with whom today I would more readily identify the poetic essence. For me, Blake is absolute. Shakespeare is richer, Milton is more sonorous, Hopkins is more sensuous—one could make many more comparative statements; but Blake has no need of qualifying epithets: he is simply poetic, in imagination and in expression.

A discovery which I then made with some of the same emotional excitement that Blake had aroused was of a contemporary poet. There was published about this time a series of small yellow chapbooks, and in it appeared the first poems of Ralph Hodgson. The poems were in harmony with the archaic style of the production: they seemed to come from a world of gypsies and highwaymen, they were sometimes sentimental, and they had a simple insistent rhythm which haunted the mind:

> Eve with her basket, was
> Deep in the bells and grass,
> Wading in bells and grass
> Up to her knees,
> Picking a dish of sweet
> Berries and plums to eat,
> Down in the bells and grass
> Under the trees.

Ralph Hodgson is a genuine poet, and I think that in spite of his sentimentality and whimsicality he has a permanent place in our literature. But he was the worst, because the most superficial kind of influence. To be influenced by Shakespeare, Milton or Wordsworth cannot do a young poet any harm: at least, it is only a very poor creature who would be influenced by their idiosyncrasies without at the same time being profitably stirred by their profundities. There is nothing profound in the poetry of Ralph Hodgson, and I am far from implying that all poetry should be profound. But just as one would feel a little silly if one found oneself unconsciously imitating the antics or gestures of another man, and tend to blame the other man for having antics and gestures of an imitable kind, so I feel inclined to criticize Hodgson's verse for its pretty jingle and infectious rhythm. These are qualities to be enjoyed by non-poetic people: the poet must go his own gait.

It is easy to retort that if a poet's genius is strong enough, his diction will be independent enough. But a poet has to undergo a process of birth and growth: he does not discover himself until he has rejected the alternative selves represented by the poetry already existing in the world. Here, perhaps, I am advancing a romantic doctrine. It is possible to conceive of poetry as an established form, and of the poet's duty as merely to add to the general fund. That is the classical conception of the poet. But my conception was, and still is, of poetry as a unique experience: the individual, with his particular moods, emotions, thoughts, trying to express himself integrally, in his own choice of words. It is true that he has to use words which are common to all his countrymen; but there is an infinite number of ways of selecting and combining these words, and from these infinite possibilities one exact, original correspondence of idea and expression must emerge, or the poem will be an affectation and a failure.

To discover what other influences were at work in this early phase of my poetic awakening, I should have to examine the verses themselves, and as I have already related, they no longer exist. But this acquisitive age actually continues until the end of my twentieth year, and for the later stage of it there is the evidence of a small 'brochure' published by Elkin Mathews in 1915 and entitled *Songs of Chaos*. An epigraph from Nietzsche—'One must have chaos within one to give birth to a dancing star'—explains the title, but this sentence which I had printed on the title-page really belongs to a later phase of my development, and the poems in the modest little volume have none of the tremendous implications of such a motto. When, in January, 1915, I joined the Army, I was posted to a battalion stationed in Dorset. I had to travel via London and arrived in that city for the first time in my life. I carried, besides my military baggage, a large bundle of poems, and at King's Cross I told the taxi-driver to go to Waterloo via Cork Street. All I knew about Mr. Mathews was that he had been publishing the kind of poetry I was interested in: I had no introduction to him nor any means of obtaining one. However, he received me very kindly in the back of his shop and undertook to consider the publication of my poems if I would pay a reader's fee, which I willingly did. A few weeks later he sent me the reader's report, which was to the effect that though the poems were too slight and imitative to be published in bulk, a small selection that would pass might be made, and he indicated the ones he thought best. I was not so much dashed by his general criticism as angry at the selection he had made. I insisted on making my own selection, and Mr. Mathews published them at my expense— I do not remember what it cost me, but it was not exorbitant.

Six months later twenty-two copies had been sold: but I had already regretted my rash and inexperienced venture, and at my request the remainder of the edition was pulped.

This abortive volume has been out of my mind for many years now, but I still possess a copy and I have unearthed it. It has the musty smell of forgotten books, but as I turn its pages I wonder if I have been too harsh with its simple conceits. I reprinted four of the poems in the 1926 edition of my *Collected Poems,* but in 1935 suppressed even these. The intensity with which I wrote some of these poems is still a vivid memory—it was not an intensity of emotion leading to expression, but an emotion generated by the act of creation. The intensity was due to the discovery that an image could be matched with exact words. The triviality of the image did not seem to matter. Even now, with all my literary and critical experience, I cannot be sure that it matters. I cannot be sure, for example, that a poem which now costs me a qualm to quote is not nevertheless a valid poem and therefore a good poem. It was called 'A Little Girl':

> I pluck a daisy here and there—
> O many a daisy do I take!
> And I string them together in a ring,
> But it's seldom the ring doesn't break.
>
> O daisies rosy, daisies white!
> If I could string them in a ring
> They'd make a bonny daisy chain—
> O why is a daisy a delicate thing?

If, as a very childlike youth, I succeeded in evoking the simplicity of a child's outlook, even a child's insight, then the result is valid. It is only sentimental if as an adult I am trying to exploit childish things.

In looking through this booklet (it ran to no more than thirty-seven pages), the only other influence besides those of Blake and Hodgson which I can now discern is that of Yeats:

> When Niordr arose from the burning deep
> And bade the waves no longer weep:—
> Niordr arose with a golden harp
> And touched the strings that never warp,
> Bidding the angry waves be still,
> And the Vanir gather to obey his will.

Niordr and the Vanir are no longer my familiar spirits, but I am reminded that at this time, at the instigation of the friend to whom I already owed so much, I read many of the Northern myths and sagas, and played with the idea of writing a Viking epic. But other influences, and other ambitions, were to intervene.

At the beginning of the Michaelmas Term, in the year 1912, I enrolled myself as a student at the University of Leeds. I was still not very certain of my intentions: ostensibly I was to become a lawyer of some kind, but secretly (it was half a secret to myself) I was determined on a literary career. I already saw myself as a novelist, a dramatist, or perhaps a journalist—the future would decide which. I was conscious of the scrappiness of my general education, and therefore resolved to spend a year in a way which was not strictly utilitarian: I took the first year course for the B.A. degree. The following year I switched over to my proper studies, which I had decided were Law and Economics,

and I was rash enough to attempt to take the two degrees
(LL.B. and B.Sc.Econ.) simultaneously. I do not think the
prescribed limits of these two curricula would have been too
much for me; but I never for a day kept within these
limits. I was an anomalous figure among my fellow-under-
graduates, whose careers were already determined: they
were going to be school-teachers, or clergymen, or practical
scientists and technicians in the local industries. Not a single
soul, so far as I ever discovered, was there for the disinterested purpose of acquiring a 'liberal' education. It is true
that I too had my purpose; but it was vague and self-selected,
and not dependent on a grant or scholarship. I could pick
and choose my subjects to suit my own idea of a career; and
I did in fact choose my subjects with an abandon which
ought undoubtedly to have been restrained. English and
French literature, Latin, Logic, Roman Law, Jurisprudence,
Common Law, Constitutional Law and History, Political
Economy, Social Economics, European History, Geology—
the mere list now makes me dizzy. The result was complete
mental congestion and over-work. My days were filled with
lectures and I read till the small hours every night. But this
is not half the toll. I had at the same time been let loose in a
library of seemingly infinite dimensions. I used to seat myself at a table in this library in every spare interval between
the lectures. By a chance which was almost perverse, the
seat to which my instinct first directed me, and which I continued to use whenever I found it free, was sheltered by a
high bookcase which contained, like a mountain veined with
shining gold, the very names with which my intellectual
curiosity was now engaged—Dostoevsky, Ibsen and Nietz-

sche. I would open my *Gaius* or *Justinian*, Welton's *Logic*
or Marshall's *Political Economy;* but soon my eyes would
be caught by the tempting titles at my side, and one by one
the volumes were drawn out and only the closing bell
awakened me from my absorption. With Dostoevsky and
Ibsen I was already partly acquainted, but Nietzsche was a
new world, and since my discovery of Blake, the most
cataclysmic. It was Nietzsche who first introduced me to
philosophy—I read far more than I could understand in his
pages, but I did not let my ignorance rest. From Nietzsche
I passed to Schopenhauer, to Kant, Hegel, Hume, Pascal,
Plato—in very much this indiscriminate order. It was as
though I had tapped a central exchange of intellectual tend-
encies; from Nietzsche communications ran in every direction and for at least five years he, and none of my professors
or friends, was my real teacher.

These years at the university were thus an orgy of acquisi-
tiveness: what basis of disciplined education had been de-
vised by the university authorities was completely swamped
by my own proclivities. It must be remembered that these
new universities have no such institution as the tutor—perhaps their greatest failing; and though I could have con-
sulted the lecturers and professors, the very oddness of my
position and the indeterminateness of my aims made this,
however desirable, not strictly necessary. And this educational machine is so rigid in its workings that any action
which is not strictly necessary is almost impossible. I remember that in my second year I did venture to send to the professor of English Literature, F. W. Moorman, two poetic
dramas which I had written in North Riding dialect—I ven-

tured to do this because he was a great enthusiast for the dialect, and perhaps the most inspiring teacher in the university. He was completely taken by surprise—though he had, some weeks earlier, been impressed by an essay I had written on Witchcraft and the Elizabethan Drama. It had never occurred to him that one of the hundred odd students who scribbled away taking notes as he lectured should attempt an original composition. He began to take a special interest in me and encouraged me to show him more of my efforts; but then came the war and before I could renew contact with this possible mentor, he had been accidentally drowned whilst bathing.

The experience of these years raises in its acutest form the whole question of disciplined education. Up to the age of fifteen my education had been perhaps more than usually disciplined, but from that age to the present day I have followed my own bent; the order has been of my own devising, and generally the order of my strongest inclinations. This is the kind of education which most authorities find reprehensible. 'I hold very strongly,' wrote Cardinal Newman in the best of all treatises on the subject, 'that the first step in intellectual training is to impress upon a boy's mind the idea of science, method, order, principle, and system; of rule and exception, of richness and harmony. . . . Let him once gain this habit of method, of starting from fixed points, of making his ground good as he goes, of distinguishing what he knows from what he does not know, and I conceive he will be gradually initiated into the largest and truest philosophical views, and will feel nothing but impatience and disgust at the random theories and imposing sophistries and dashing paradoxes, which carry away half-formed and superficial intellects.' These words, in which I recognize a large measure of truth, are a complete condemnation of the method of education which I pursued, and yet I am not entirely repentant. Admittedly I had some good habits: what I read I tended to read thoroughly; I made notes and to the best of my unaided ability made the ground good as I went on my way. Nietzsche is not a starting-point that Newman would have approved—he would almost certainly have included his works among 'the random theories and imposing sophistries and dashing paradoxes' which he scorns, and my intellect among the half-formed and superficial which are carried away by such theories and sophistries. Nevertheless, Nietzsche *was* a starting-point and all the circumstances considered, not one which I regret. He gave me vistas which were quite outside the range of formal education; he introduced me to the ferment of the contemporary ideas. In his company I knew the excitement of an intellectual adventure, that highest exaltation which only comes when truth is conceived as a fleeting quarry in whose pursuit the whole mind must be engaged.

In my subsequent years I was often to come into contact with great men whose intellects had been formed in the gradual and disciplined manner indicated by Newman. Let me admit that I have always felt in their presence a sense of weakness; but it is the weakness of the runner who has returned from the chase and found the imperturbable god of reason still changeless in his niche. I had felt the earth spinning underneath my feet, and the clouds racing me in the sky; beauty had stirred like an animal in the covert and my senses had been assailed from a thousand directions. The flush on my features was a reflexion of the animation in my mind, where the images were as vivid as nature and as restless as the sea. If my ideal had been a static form, then I should have withered like a wreath at the feet of this impassive god; but my ideal was a labile green shoot, an emergent new world, a manifestation of the unknown in the desert of dead facts.

I have found that most people whose minds have responded to a formal university education are like monoliths. They are bodies at rest. They have acquired during their university years a choice armory of information, and they assume that it will serve them for the rest of their lives. Many of them sell their classics to the second-hand bookseller before they 'come down' from Oxford or Cambridge; or if they keep them, it is for the sake of sentimental associations. They are stored in a glazed bookcase behind the 'chesterfield,' with a college shield on the wall above and a tobacco-jar on the ledge. In a few years the once proud possessor of a first in Greats will have forgotten all but a few tags of his Greek and Latin, and will be reduced to defending a classical education for its supposed disciplinary virtues. He can boast of having 'done' his Plato or his Aristotle, his Aeschylus or his Euripides; but these are names now, mingled with his sentimental recollections of professors and dons. They had not become a part of his life, a continuing influence and ever-present inspiration. They and the whole galaxy of classical poets and philosophers are dead and distant worlds.

There is another side to the argument. Some of these

formally educated young men, on leaving the universities, have gone into the Civil Service or business, and have become very efficient administrators. Between their present efficiency and their education there is a very direct relation: not the relation of a vocational training to the vocation pursued (which is much more the ideal of the modern universities and technical colleges), but a relation sanctioned by the intangible virtues of 'character'—in Newman's words, 'the force, the steadiness, the comprehensiveness and the versatility of intellect, the command over our own powers, the instinctive just estimate of things as they pass before us, which sometimes indeed is a natural gift, but commonly is not gained without much effort and the exercise of years.' These are the virtues which are needed in the upper ranks of any social hierarchy—these virtues rather than specialized knowledge or technical skill—and the Civil Service has quite rightly rejected the notion of a particularized training such as the Army, the Navy and the professions require. Its flexibility, its adaptability, its very humanity depend on this paradox in its recruitment.

The ideals of this kind of education are generally summed up in the word 'character,' though latterly the more equivocal word 'leadership' has been used. But administration is not the only function of an educated man, nor is leadership a necessity in a community of free individuals. There is an alternative ideal of education, for which I have always attempted to reserve the word 'personality.' Character is the product of a disciplined education: discipline inculcates habits of mind as well as of body, and the result is a firm, dependable set of ideas and reactions upon which a definite type of society can be based. A character is not necessarily conservative: rather it is constructive, and in a time of stress or disintegration might well seem revolutionary. It is moral, though its morality is not necessarily conventional. It cultivates a 'taste,' but this taste is rational rather than aesthetic, retrospective and historical rather than experimental and contemporary.

A personality, on the other hand, is distinguished by immediacy and by what I would call lability, or the capacity to change without loss of integrity. Keats, who discerned the quality in himself, gave it the name of Negative Capability; and in Hamlet Shakespeare depicted the type in all its mutability.

Character is only attained by limitation. The senses, which would otherwise be open to the impact of every phenomenal event, must be canalized, protected by a hard cortex or shell, and only allowed to operate when they have been directed by the conscious will; and it can be argued that sensations and their attendant emotions are all the finer for being thus restricted. But the personality will have none of this arbitrary interference with the natural process of selectivity: the senses are open to every impression which falls upon them, and the mind surrenders to its environment. Admittedly, from a moral and social point of view, there is a danger that such a passive attitude will lead to instability and disintegration. But the values of the personality are neither moral nor social: they are religious or aesthetic. Here the word 'religious,' put in contrast to 'moral,' may cause some surprise; but I would be prepared to maintain that the essentially religious experience described by the great mystics of the East as well as the West, and now generally known in modern theology as the Kierkegaardian 'instant,' the Barthian 'crisis' or 'leap,' is a surrender of the existential being only possible to a personality, a man of negative capability.

To question the values of the personality, therefore, is to question the values of mysticism and of art. The greatest mistake would be to suppose that a society can be based exclusively on one type of human being. Society needs for vitality, and for effective progress, the contrast and opposition of types, more particularly of these two fundamental types which I have called characters and personalities. The tautness of the social fabric depends on their dialectical counterplay.

It would seem to follow from these considerations that there should be two systems of education, one for character and one for personality. That would obviously be impracticable, and the most we can hope for is an elasticity in the general system which would provide for both types of individual. The present system is directed almost exclusively to the creation of character, and at its best is very successful in this aim. The survival of personality in this system is a matter of chance: sometimes an understanding teacher will give his protection to a boy obviously not made for the mold; but more often the boy revolts and escapes from the system (as Shelley did), or by some chance is never submitted to it—is *privately* educated, as we say. My own case was still more exceptional: I entered the system as a casual and undirected unit, a misfit. I did not consciously reject the system: rather, it rejected me. I played the game, but I did not obey the rules. I did not conform to a regular routine, and before I could be punished for my dilettantism, the war had taken me to another and a more realistic school.

During the whole of this subsequent period I read avidly. Even in the most difficult circumstances—in the most desperate trench warfare—I was never without a book in my pocket. It was necessarily very unsystematic reading, but it included Henry James and Flaubert, Baudelaire and Rimbaud, Plato and Berkeley. But it is not really necessary to isolate this period: I would rather say that the process of self-education was uninterrupted by the war, the only difference being that before and after that event I was better equipped to find or refer to the books of which day by day I became conscious.

*   *   *

I have not lost sight of the original purpose of this chapter, which was to relate my gradual discovery of the world of poetry. But a divagation has been necessary to show what part was played in the process by my education. I think I have shown that it was mainly negative. When I look back on this period of my life, and when I compare my experience with that of other people, my strongest feeling is one of relief. It is so easy to crush a nascent sensibility, or if not to crush it, then to deform it. The poetic sensibility is especially vulnerable, and especially in England. Socially the poet is despised: for the great majority of people he is merely a comic figure, the butt of *Punch* and the music-halls. Poetry as an art has become a secret and shame-faced activity: people are even shy of being seen reading poetry in a train, whereas the public declamation of poetry, as it was practised even in the nineteenth century, and as it is still practised in Russia, is quite unknown.* Attempts to re-introduce the art through the very suitable medium of broadcasting have so far been very disappointing.

If this social opposition to poetry is reinforced by what one might call a process of academic sterilization, it is very diffi-cult to retain any trace of free sensibility. Actually the attempt to reduce an art to materia paedagogii is always fatal: poetry cannot be dissected unless it is first killed. I do not imply, however, that poetry—or art in general—should be excluded from the curriculum of our schools and uni-versities. On the contrary, I think that the arts should play a greater part in education. But they should be treated as arts and not as 'subjects,' still less as sciences. This is not the place to enlarge on the question, but as a general indication

---

* A few years ago I was one of a group of English poets invited to the Russian Embassy to meet three Russian poets (Lugovskoy, Selvinsky and one whose name I have forgotten). After tea and vodka, we adjourned to a drawing-room where our Russian col-leagues recited in turn their own poems, magnificently. Though few, if any, of us knew the language, we were made to feel its music and its passion, and even the meaning penetrated by virtue of the poets' mime and rhetoric. When they had finished, they turned to us and asked us to recite some of our famous English poetry to them. We looked at each other in nervous embarrassment. After much shuffling and modest protestation, an elderly poet began to pipe out Shelley's 'Ode to the West Wind' in a high monotonous voice; faltered and broke down. Someone else recited a little poem about a little bird. There were a few other irrelevancies and then we parted, feeling that we had betrayed, not only our country, but also the art for which our country is respected even when all our other qualities are despised.

of what I mean, I would say that it is necessary to make a clear separation of the historical and the technical aspects of each art. The history of literature or the history of painting (including, of course, the history of their technical development) would be distinct subjects, taught like the history of any other aspect of social evolution. But the technique of literature, like the technique of painting, would be encouraged as a practical activity. Poetry and plays would be written, recited or produced, and the creative artist would be elevated above the academic scholar. It would, of course, revolutionize educational standards if marks were to be awarded, or even a degree granted, on the artistic merits of an original composition; but that, I contend, is the only way in which the arts can be brought into organic relation with a vital system of education.

Otherwise, it is better to let the aesthetic impulse develop unaided, as it did in my own case. Once I had become aware of this creative impulse in myself, I needed no encouragement to educate myself in the subject. I was filled with an insatiable curiosity which extended to all the poetry of the past, to the poetry of other languages, and to the poetry of my contemporaries. In a few years I had raced through all the poetry in my own language which I thought likely to appeal to me, and was then eager to discover the poetry of France, of Italy and of Germany. I doubt if I should ever have attempted to learn the languages of these countries but for the curiosity engendered by my poetic impulse. Latin poetry had been almost completely destroyed for me by the education I had received in this subject, but a measure of enjoyment was preserved in poets who by chance had never been 'set,' such as Catullus and Lucretius. But I must confess that Latin poetry in general has played an insignificant part in my poetic experience. I have excused myself by supposing a lack of sympathy, but this lack may have been due to a deficiency of knowledge. For Greek poetry, however, I have felt much sympathy on the basis of no knowledge at all. I have never had the time, nor perhaps the will, to teach myself Greek, and Greek poetry, in its essential nature, remains unknown to me. I say 'in its essential nature' because it is only in translation that I have read the great classics of Greek poetry; and though this may have given me a certain insight into the Greek spirit, it is futile, as I know from my experience with foreign poetry in general, to pretend that my lips have even touched the rim of the hippocrene fountain. I console myself with the thought that I am still far from the age at which Cato first learned the language.

In this account of my discovery of poetry I have so far not gone beyond Blake and Yeats. I have mentioned Ralph Hodgson, but his influence was short-lived and superficial. The next stage is represented by Donne and Browning among the poets of the past, and by a group of contemporary poets known as the Imagists. Together, these two influences may be said to have completed my poetic education. The years to follow held such surprises as Rimbaud and Apollinaire, Hölderlin and Rilke, but though such poets have deepened my conception of the content of poetry, they have not altered the attitude to the problems of technique which I formed under the influence of the Imagists.

Donne is an influence apart—not in any sense a technical

influence, but rather an extension of sensibility, an education in emotional rectitude. The conceits which so disgusted Johnson appealed to me because they were an attempt to bridge the separate worlds of intellect and feeling, and I began to conceive of poetry as an intermediary between these conflicting forces. But it never occurred to me that poets of the twentieth century should use the language and diction of the seventeenth century—they might, with as good reason, dress in the costumes of that period. There was something even in this respect to learn from Donne: he did, after all, refuse to sacrifice his meaning to a conventional ideal of smoothness (which is not the same thing as felicity). Browning's technique I found entirely relevant. He too was occupied by this problem—the expression of intellectual concepts in the language of feeling—though his intelligence was historical and ethical rather than experimental and aesthetic, and his emotions were distorted by the moral conventions of his age. His technique, however, was free: a reaction against the Parnassian polish of Tennyson and Arnold, a return to the rugged exactitude of Donne. Until Hopkins was discovered (in 1918, though odd poems had appeared earlier) Browning was the only English poet of the immediate past who worked as anything like a ferment in the minds of the poets of the decade 1906–1915 (the decisive years in the formation of the modern poetic tradition in England). There was also Yeats, but he did not then appear as of the past: he was one of our contemporaries, himself subject to some of the same influences. But even Yeats can to a great extent be discounted—his real influence came later, when his later poems grew realistic and political,

and as such appealed to a still later generation. Even before
the outbreak of the war, we distrusted Yeats's romanticism.
Only the Irish could move freely in the Celtic twilight,
though the Americans might assimilate it like any other
foreign tradition, and it was the Americans among us, particularly Ezra Pound, who paid most respect to it. For the
Anglo-Saxons it might be a fashionable craze, but as a poetic
style it was racially foreign to us, only to be adopted as a
mannerism and an affectation. The war finally killed it. An
epigraph which appeared next to the title-page of the first
edition of my war-poems, *Naked Warriors,* was intended
as a parody of Yeats, and as a cynical expression of my own
disillusionment:

> War through my soul has driven
> its jagged blades:
> The riven
> dream fades—
>> So you'd better grieve, heart, in the gathering night,
>> Grieve, heart, in the loud twilight.

What I wish to insist on is the importance of Browning in
the pre-war years. It is only necessary to turn to the poems
published by Ezra Pound—'il miglior fabbro' of us all—
particularly the volumes *Personae* and *Exultations,* to see
that influence predominant. Even when Pound is writing a
poem with a Provençal or Romantic theme, it may be given
the manner or diction of Browning. The same influence is
not absent from the earlier poems of his friend T. S. Eliot.

Mr. Pound, I know, has many other gods—Fenollosa and
Rémy de Gourmont, for example—and he is very jealous on
their behalf. But I am not writing about critical influences,

which were very various, but of direct mentors of the technique and diction of verse. The modification of Browning's influence came from France—from Rimbaud and Laforgue, and from the early verse of Duhamel, Jules Romains, Jean de Bosschère, André Spire and Apollinaire. There was also T. E. Hulme, but by now his five short poems have begun to assume rather too much prominence in the history of this period. They were certainly good textbook examples of imagist technique, but if Hulme had written fifty or a hundred poems as good, we should not have heard so much about them.

This explanation has been long enough, and I must pick up the residue of my own impressions. If Browning was the last of my historical discoveries, it will now be seen how he came to be fused in my imagination with the activities of a contemporary school which was at that time learning from Browning and applying his technique to the expression of a modern sensibility. I had now reached the vanguard of the art for which I had felt an affinity in my own being. Henceforth my discovery of poetry was to be directed by my passionate participation in its immediate destiny. Hitherto I had read for enjoyment and understanding: I was now to read as if I drew in the substance of life itself, creatively manifested in the minds of living poets.

From this experience, which lasted from the year 1913 to 1917, I quickly evolved what I would have called my philosophy of composition. There was a general feeling then that some new philosophy was necessary, much as it had been necessary when Wordsworth and Coleridge published their *Lyrical Ballads* in 1798, and several attempts to formulate one had been made by the young poets for whom I felt such a strong sympathy. The clearest statement of these years is the Preface to *Some Imagist Poets,* an anthology published in 1915 which included the work of Richard Aldington, H.D., F. S. Flint, and D. H. Lawrence. That preface still remains the locus classicus for the doctrines of the imagist school, and since it is not now generally available, I will quote the six 'common principles' * which it set forth:

1. To use the language of common speech, but to employ always the *exact* word, not the nearly-exact, nor the merely decorative word.

2. To create new rhythms—as the expression of new moods —and not to copy old rhythms, which merely echo old moods. We do not insist upon 'free-verse' as the only method of writing poetry. We fight for it as for a principle of liberty. We believe that the individuality of a poet may often be better expressed in free-verse than in conventional forms. In poetry, a new cadence means a new idea.

3. To allow absolute freedom in the choice of subject. It is not good art to write badly about aeroplanes and automobiles; nor is it necessarily bad art to write about the past. We believe passionately in the artistic value of modern life, but we wish to point out that there is nothing so uninspiring nor so old-fashioned as an aeroplane of the year 1911.

4. To present an image (hence the name: 'Imagist'). We

---

* The best *defence* of these principles is F. S. Flint's Preface to *Otherworld,* a volume of 'cadences' published in 1920 (Poetry Bookshop) and dedicated, I am proud to recall, to me. Flint had far more to do with the development of the Imagist school than has generally been acknowledged.

are not a school of painters, but we believe that poetry should render particulars exactly and not deal in vague generalities, however magnificent and sonorous. It is for this reason that we oppose the cosmic poet, who seems to us to shirk the real difficulties of his art.

5. To produce poetry that is hard and clear, never blurred nor indefinite.

6. Finally, most of us believe that concentration is of the very essence of poetry.

Three years later, in the third number of *Art and Letters,* I published my own 'Definitions towards a Modern Theory of Poetry.' I began with the following 'axioms':

1. Form is determined by the emotion which requires expression.

Corollary: Form is not an unchanging mold into which any emotion can be poured.

2. The poem is an artistic whole demanding strict unity.

3. The criterion of the poem is the quality of the vision expressed, granted that the expression is adequate.

Corollary: Rhyme, meter, cadence, alliteration, are various decorative devices to be used as the vision demands, and are not formal quantities pre-ordained.

I was evidently reading Spinoza at the time, and the whole essay is written in a dry analytical style. Terms like 'vision,' 'emotion,' 'value,' 'unity,' and 'form' are defined with the aid of a psychological jargon which I should now try to avoid; but the essay, differently worded, would still represent my views on the theory of poetry. What interests me now is to find myself criticizing my friends the Imagists. I admitted that they were the only modern school of poets which showed 'any clarity of creative intention'; but I criticized them because 'in their manifestoes they had renounced the decorative word, but their sea-violets and wild hyacinths tend to become as decorative as the beryls and jades of Oscar Wilde.' I also accused them of lacking 'that aesthetic selection which is the artist's most peculiar duty' —by which I meant, as far as I can now make out, that they thought any passing mood or emotion worthy of poetic expression—they did not apply an aesthetic (or did I mean intellectual?) judgment to the quality of the emotion itself. I concluded: 'Modern England may be "a nest of singing birds," but it is well for us to realize that the poem is still rather a primitive affair, and to make it otherwise there is a call for stern artistic devotion. We must shrink from the exotic and the decadent, and from the sheltered garden of cultivated beauties. Beauty is a discipline, demanding all the intensity of a man's intelligence to present clear and undefiled the infinite quality in things. The artist's vision is the supreme value; the expression of it is the supreme difficulty.'

This essay must have been written early in 1918, that is to say, before the end of the war, though I cannot remember where or in what circumstances I wrote it. I can look back with amusement on its earnest solemnity now, but I think it reflects something of the contradiction that was being forced on us by our daily experience. We were trying to maintain an abstract aesthetic ideal in the midst of terrorful and inhuman events. In my own case I am certain that this devotion to abstract notions and intellectual reveries saved me from a raw reaction to these events. But as the war went on, year after year, and there seemed no escape from its indignity except death, some compromise between dream and reality became necessary. The only worthy compromise, I even then dimly realized, was a synthesis—some higher reality in which the freedom of the mind and the necessity of experience became reconciled. If I had been older that solution might have been a philosophy; but I was not contemplative enough for that, nor wise enough. I therefore sought the solution in art: in a poetry which would represent my aesthetic ideals and yet at the same time deal with the experience that threatened to overwhelm me. The result was a series of war poems, some of which I afterwards destroyed, but most of which I published in a small volume to which I gave the title *Naked Warriors*. (Incidentally, I am sure that I had not at that time seen Pollaiuolo's engraving which so perfectly illustrates the title and the epigraph which I put on the title-page: 'And there were some that went into the battle naked and unarmed, fighting only with the fervor of their spirit, dying and getting many wounds.') It may seem that this was but a feeble response to such an immense event. In a later chapter I shall discuss my reactions to war in more detail, but on this level of aesthetic response, I would ask the reader to reflect on the millions who were engaged in that conflict and then to examine its poetic aftermath in any of the languages of the nations engaged. It is infinitesimal in quantity and almost negligible in poetic quality. Many years later, in his Introduction to the *Oxford Book of Modern Verse,* Yeats was to offer a reason for this strange disparity—'the same reason that made Arnold withdraw his "Empedocles on Etna" from circulation; passive suffering is not a theme for poetry'; and for the same reason

Yeats decided to exclude war poetry from his anthology. It was a judgment that was to arouse a good deal of resentment among the young poets of today, and I am not sure that I myself accept it—at least, not for the reason given. Another sentence in the same paragraph of Yeats's Introduction, though it is metaphorical, seems to me to be nearer the truth of the matter: 'When man has withdrawn into the quick-silver at the back of the mirror no great event becomes luminous in his mind. . . .' In other words, the necessary element is the time-lapse implicit in Wordsworth's phrase, 'recollected in tranquillity,' an element of 'aesthetic distance.' Even passive suffering can be a fit theme for poetry if it is seen objectively enough, against a wide background. The direct expression of suffering is an animal cry; poetry, too, is an animal cry, but of another kind. There is a difference which is the difference between the scream of a slaughtered pig and the song of a nightingale, and this is perhaps the difference between passive suffering and passive joy. But art begins—and I think this was Yeats's meaning—when the joy is purposive, an active sublimation even of suffering and tragedy.

In 1917 and 1918, in the intervals of leave from the Front, I gradually made the acquaintance of the poets whose work I admired—Flint, Aldington, Pound and Eliot—and met other writers with whom I was in sympathy, such as A. R. Orage and P. Wyndham Lewis. Influences which had been literary and indirect now became personal, and the cold communication of the page was exchanged for the intimate give-and-take of conversation. Some of these friendships were to endure without interruption to the present day, some became intermittent, some never developed at all. It is not my intention to discuss my personal relationships in this book, but I cannot avoid a reference to my friendship with Eliot, because it has certainly had a considerable effect on my intellectual development, perhaps just because we are so divergent in origin, education, character and ideals. He has called himself royalist, classicist, and anglo-catholic, whereas I (with qualifications similar to those he made) would call myself anarchist, romanticist and agnostic. A long and uninterrupted friendship has been possible because in spite of these divergences, we have always agreed about things which are perhaps finally more important: the sense of beauty in poetry, the quality of the expression of ideas, and the priority to be given to natural goodness even when the intelligence seems perverse. I think our friendship has a certain general significance, because too much importance, in history and criticism, is given to ideological similarities and not enough to human sympathies. Life, even in its intimate or arcane recesses, is still dialectical.

These friendships no doubt modified my poetic outlook, but I think I may say that by the end of the war I had discovered myself and my style—that is to say, I had made an equation between emotion and image, between feeling and expression. So long as I was true to this equation, I need not be afraid of influences or acquired mannerisms. Poetry was reduced to an instrument of precision. 'Reduced' will imply, of course, a lack of bulk: from that time my output of verse was to be severely restricted. But what I wrote I tended to keep: I no longer destroyed a large part of my writing. Criticism had become innate, composition an instinctive language; and though I am very far from claiming perfection or permanence for the poems I have retained, I do not think it will be necessary for a reader of the future to approach my work with squared shoulders: he can accept or reject me on the instant. By this statement I lay myself open to the charge that there is nothing in my poetry to detain the reader; but that, of course, is not what I mean. One of the essential characteristics of poetry is what Coleridge called 'the power of reducing multitude into unity of effect.' Whatever the nature of poetry, be it lyrical or dramatic, meditative or philosophical, this unity of effect should exist, and be immediately apparent. If that unity is achieved, the poem has that quality which is possessed by all true works of art—the quality of retaining our interest in spite of familiarity.

Here I will break off this account of my discovery of poetry—'break off' because it is an enterprise which still continues. I am not now likely to modify my own technique, and I have reached that becalmed stage of life, midway between youth and old age, in which the poetic impulse is often dormant. But I still retain the zest, the insatiable thirst for this pellucid essence of experience. All other sensuous experiences are as nothing to this perception of poetic beauty. A few years ago I took my son, then aged about eleven, to an open-air performance of *A Midsummer Night's Dream*. It was a brilliant sunny day, and everywhere, not least on the green and leafy stage, the atmosphere was gay. But time after time the impact of Shakespeare's words—the words themselves and not their meaning—would send a gush of tears to my eyes, and there was no darkness to hide my paradoxical visage from my neighbors. But they too were absorbed in the play—some in the antics, some in the atmosphere; some few in the cadence of the words that came winged with inexplicable sorrow through the summer air.

3

THE TREE OF LIFE

IN 'The Innocent Eye' I have already given some idea of
the atmosphere of simple piety which surrounded me in
my early years. My father was not emotional in his religion;
he was a strict Christian and a man of natural, equable
goodness. Only a blizzard would have prevented him from
driving the five miles to church every Sunday. Night and
morning we said our prayers before our parents; there were
frequent readings from the Bible, and as soon as we were
old enough we had to learn the Collect for the day. All this
was part of our routine, with no trace of effort or self-
consciousness; and since it was also part of the routine of
the few houses we entered, it never occurred to me to question it. When, at the age of ten, I went away to school,
there was a very different atmosphere, but no essential
change of practice. The headmaster was again a man of
simple natural piety, and he communicated his spirit to the
whole school. There were daily prayers after breakfast in
the dining-room; and every evening each boy knelt down
by the side of his bed. The most violent change was the
Sunday service. The school had been founded by pious Con-
gregationalists, and it was to a Congregational chapel in the

town that we trooped each Sunday—the older boys to the evening as well as the morning service. It was inevitable that I should feel a little chilled by the bleaker atmosphere of these conventicles. The atmosphere I was used to was not luxurious; but at least it was romantic; and there is no romance in varnished pine, hygienic distemper, or stenciled friezes. The singing at Kirkdale had been exiguous and toneless; it was now hearty and voluminous, but our voices did not chime in. The brief homilies which even a child could understand had become interminable moral discourses punctured, more often than not, by a boy's fainting. Never, during the five years at school, did I or any other boy that I knew of, question the religious discipline which was imposed on us. But the routine was no longer accepted instinctively. We all hated the church parade, the crocodile march, the fight against the fidgets or the giggles. Our real piety, if we possessed any, was reserved for our private prayers before going to bed.

When I left school, at the age of fifteen, a great change took place. For the first time I became consciously religious. I naturally returned to the Church of England, and attended the services regularly. Though the prosperous suburban church to which I went had none of the primitive poetry of Kirkdale, it was romantic in its neo-gothic way, and worked on my boyish imagination. I was swept away, as boys often are at this age, on a wave of devotional ecstasy. Ecstasy is perhaps a magniloquent word to describe my feelings, but I want to convey the irrational nature of this phase. It preceded the discovery of philosophy to which I have already referred; it was not accompanied by any conscious thought on the problems of religion, nor indeed on any problem, unless it were that of social conduct. It was manifested, firstly in an intensity of prayer; further, in a scrupulous attendance at public worship; and finally in a kind of dazed exaltation during public worship. I did not sing nor even repeat the litany or creed: rather I would fix my gaze on some one point—the face of the preacher, a lamp or a candle-flame—and by concentration exclude all other sensations. My whole being would hang on this bright point, whilst around me swirled the music of the organ, the voice of the preacher, the soaring gothic arches. In this way I no doubt felt that I was bringing my consciousness nearer to a perception of the glory of God. But it was a fruitless and insubstantial practice, from which I gained only a kind of religiosity, and no strength of mind or grace of virtue. But it is possibly a practice indulged in by other devotees, whose religion lies more in the regions of hypnotic ritualism than of true devotion.

This phase lasted for at the most two years. I passed out of it gradually, and as a result of my own development, without persuasion of any kind. It was a misfortune that the seeds of skepticism began to germinate at the very moment the necessity of confirmation was being pressed on me. This ceremony had been delayed until my brother had left school, and it was my mother's desire that we should be confirmed together. The vicar of the parish in which we then lived was approached and agreed to give us special preparation. He was a venerable old man, of some reputation as a preacher. I am afraid he found us dull and uncomprehending novices.

I had now reached a stage of doubt which completely paralyzed my mind. I did not dare to confess my thoughts, much less to reveal my skepticism. I did not wish to distress my mother, nor mislead my brother. I went on with the painful farce and reached such a stage of mental confusion that at the end of the preparation I could not even repeat the Creed without error: without conviction, my mind could not memorize the meaningless succession of syllables. But in due course I was confirmed and for some months went to Communion with my mother and brother. Then came the first year at the university, and the open access to the very fount of heresy. I could no longer endure the falsity of my position. First I gave up my prayers and then my attendance at church. My mother was both grieved and baffled, and in vain brought to bear upon me the influence of relatives and friends. But my unbelief was now too positive: I had to persist or resign all faith in myself. I brought much unhappiness upon myself and upon others: my mother was ill and shortly to die. But the dark struggle brought no other issue. And in that state of unbelief I have remained until the present day.

I purposely use this word 'unbelief' (it is the word used by the father of the dumb child in that tragic prayer: 'Lord, I believe; help Thou mine unbelief') because it best describes the purely neutral or agnostic state of my mind. I have never adopted an attitude of active disbelief. It has never occurred to me to proselytize on behalf of rationalism or atheism. Indeed, I have always had the greatest respect for genuinely religious people, and many of my best friends, with whom I am in closest mutual sympathy, are devout Christians. This fact, together with my intellectual interest in religion, and at one time my frequent references to scholasticism, has often led to the assumption that I was at least in sympathy with the Catholic Church, and perhaps a neo-Thomist. It is very possible that if I had been born in France rather than England, I should have been drawn into one or other of those Catholic groups which seem to be able to reconcile an intellectual support of the Catholic faith with a complete disregard of, and even contempt for, the Catholic hierarchy. But even that is doubtful. The state of unbelief to which I refer cannot possibly lead to any positive action, least of all to political activity.

Intellectual vanity is most often the charge brought against this state of mind, but I do not think it is really justified. If I had had any clue to the universe to offer as an alternative to theocracy; if I had been a materialist and thought that all the phenomena of our human nature could be explained by means of the various physical sciences; or even if I had consciously deliberated on the different explanations of the universe offered by the religions and philosophies of the world, it would have been a different matter. Then I should have been pitting my individual intelligence against the traditional and relatively universal intelligence of the Church into which I was born. Naturally my state of mind has been influenced and even induced by intellectual considerations, and it is a genuine puzzle to me how anyone with a knowledge of the comparative history of religions can retain an *exclusive* belief in the tenets of his particular sect. But I have generally kept my bewilderment to myself, and since I am willing to admit the inexplicability of the universe and of our human destiny, it is not difficult to accommodate myself to minor mysteries of this sort. I suspect that actually we all construct our private myths, and that even the members of a dogmatic church, if they have any imagination at all, elaborate a separate fantasy from the symbols and ideas which are communicated to them. An agnostic can acquiesce in such an individual solution, reserving his criticism for the structures of temporal power to which the individual illogically surrenders his intellectual will, his rational and moral science.*

The fundamental consideration in our attitude to religion is not intellectual, and cannot therefore be a question of vanity or pride. In most cases it seems to be nothing but the fear, conscious or subconscious, of death. The great majority of men cannot bear to contemplate a universe in which their individual existence is strictly limited, their life a *little* life 'rounded with a sleep.' They cling desperately to the conception of an after-life, and since the decay and disappearance of the physical body is an only too evident fact, they are compelled to postulate a non-material after-life, a spiritual immortality. Once this postulate is made, it is elaborated: the spiritual life after death is given its hierarchy on the analogy of the life on earth, and a being commanding this hierarchy, and logically the whole process of the universe, completes

---

* 'The excellence of religion is due to an idealization of experience which, while making religion noble if treated as poetry, makes it necessarily false if treated as science. Its function is rather to draw from reality materials for an image of that ideal to which reality ought to conform, and make us citizens, by anticipation, in the world we crave.'—SANTAYANA: *Interpretations of Poetry and Religion*, p. vi.

the fantasy. The history of religion in the modern world is the history of the various attempts made by mankind to substantiate this particular fantasy, to give it realistic validity and material evidence. So passionately have men desired to preserve this illusion that they have devoted their best mental energies to its philosophical justification, with the consequence that the world of thought outside the churches cannot compare in depth of feeling or beauty of expression with the art and philosophy inspired by religion. It is true that a great poet like Shakespeare cannot be claimed by any of the churches; but neither can he be convincingly claimed by any brand of heresy or paganism. His sympathetic insight hovers over every manifestation of the human spirit.

My own attitude towards death has never been one of fear —I should say, never one of overt fear, because I cannot be sure of what is going on below the surface of my consciousness. When I first became aware of the brevity of life, my feelings were of anger and resentment. Soon afterwards, when I became a soldier on active service, death was no longer an abstract and relatively distant prospect, but an imminent possibility. But just before I went to the Front, death had robbed me of my mother, and that event had shaken me to the depth of my being. So strong was the psychic shock that when I found myself in a strange country and amidst new surroundings, I began to be haunted by such vivid dreams that for months I existed in a state of uncertainty. Was she really dead? Or had her death occurred only in one of my obsessive nightmares? I did not dare to

THE TREE OF LIFE

give expression to this real state of uncertainty, but as the
months passed, there came no confirmation of her existence.
Meanwhile death was being forced more brutally into my
consciousness: men were being killed by my side, before my
eyes. The terrible fragility of life was made evident to me;
I saw that individuality and intelligence and all the unique
make of a man could seep into the ground with a trickle of
warm blood. But still I did not fear death, strongly as I
wanted to live. The philosophy which was forced on me by
this experience was simply fatalistic—it was not resigned
enough to be called stoical. It had in it an element of bitterness or resentment which we find in 'the tragic view of life,'
and fatalism is perhaps the best word to describe my permanent attitude to this problem. My favorite symbol is the
Tree of Life. The human race is the trunk and branches of
this tree, and individual men are the leaves which appear
one season, flourish for a summer, and then die. I am like a
leaf of this tree, and one day I shall be torn off by a storm or
simply decay and fall, and become a pinch of compost about
its roots. But meanwhile I am conscious of the tree's flowing
sap and steadfast strength. Deep down in my consciousness
is the consciousness of a collective life, a life of which I am a
part and to which I contribute a minute but unique extension. When I die and fall, the tree remains, nourished to
some small degree by my brief manifestation of life. Millions
of leaves have preceded me and millions will follow me; the
tree itself grows and endures.

Some people can find no consolation in this symbol. They
are the people who fear death—who can only die comfort-

ably in the illusion that they will continue to live in another world or on another plane of consciousness. If they can really maintain such an illusion, they are welcome to it; I have no wish to deprive them of it, but in my own philosophy I cannot tolerate any element which might be self-deception.

There is a passage in the Taoist classic, *Chuang Tzu,* which perfectly expresses the attitude towards death which circumstances forced me to adopt thus early in my life. It has been beautifully translated into English by Arthur Waley:

When Chuang Tzu's wife died, the logician Hui Tzu came to the house to join in the rites of mourning. To his astonishment he found Chuang Tzu sitting with an inverted bowl on his knees, drumming upon it and singing a song. 'After all,' said Hui Tzu, 'she lived with you, brought up your children, grew old along with you. That you should not mourn for her is bad enough; but to let your friends find you drumming and singing—that is really going too far!' 'You misjudge me,' said Chuang Tzu. 'When she died, I was in despair, as any man well might be. But soon, pondering on what had happened, I told myself that in death no strange new fate befalls us. In the beginning we lack not life only, but form. Not form only, but spirit. We are blent in the one great featureless, indistinguishable mass. Then a time came when the mass evolved spirit, spirit evolved form, form evolved life. And now life in its turn has evolved death. For not nature only but man's being has its seasons, its sequence of spring and autumn, summer and winter. If someone is tired and has gone to lie down, we do not pursue him with shouting and bawling. She whom I have lost has lain down to sleep for a while in the Great Inner Room. To break in upon her rest with the noise of lamentation would show that I knew nothing of nature's Sovereign Law.' *

'This attitude towards death,' Waley remarks, 'is but part of a general attitude towards the universal laws of nature, which is one not merely of resignation nor even of acquiescence, but a lyrical, almost ecstatic acceptance which has inspired some of the most moving passages in Taoist literature. That we should question nature's right to make and unmake, that we should hanker after some role that nature did not intend us to play is not merely futile, not merely damaging to that tranquility of the "spirit" which is the essence of Taoism, but involves, in view of our utter helplessness, a sort of fatuity at once comic and disgraceful.' I like to think that I too possess something of this general attitude towards the universal laws of nature, something of the Taoist tranquility of the 'spirit.' I have been familiar with a translation of the *Tao Tê Ching* for many years, but it is only lately, under the guidance of Arthur Waley's books, that I have become acquainted with the main tenets of Taoism, and discovered how closely, and with how many facets, it embodies the truths towards which I have stumbled since I first began to think about the problems of life. It would be absurd to describe myself as a Taoist, because the idiom in which this philosophy of life is expressed is an alien one, colored by the circumstances and customs of a distant time and land. But Christianity, in its primitive form, is not dissimilar,

* *Chuang Tzu* XVIII, 2. From *The Way and Its Power* (London, 1934), pp. 53-4.

and embodies not a little of the same tradition. If an Anglo-Saxon of the twentieth century can accept the gospel of a Nazarene whose birth is chosen to mark the beginning of our era, would it be any less strange to find an appropriate philosophy of life in the sayings of a Chinese sage who lived a few centuries earlier? But actually I have not sought out this philosophy, to adopt it. My attitude was inherent in my personality, and was brought to expression by self-examination in the light of experience. An 'influence' is as easily shed as it is acquired. It is not teachers that we should seek, but exemplars who confirm and strengthen the truth we have discovered in ourselves.

I have confessed that I only discovered the Taoist comparatively recently. I do not think it is likely now that I shall fundamentally modify my philosophy of life, but it may be of some interest to cast a backward glance over the stages of my development. In doing so, a distinction must be made between intellectual and philosophical interests—at least, the enthusiasm generated by various writers falls into two separate categories. My early enthusiasm for Nietzsche, for example, was purely intellectual: my life was unaffected —I never became a Nietzschean, either in thought or deed. Similarly, philosophers like Plato and Spinoza, both of whom I have read with absorption and sympathy, have never been a part of my intimate existence. I remember that I once tried to adopt *The Republic* as a pocket companion, but though I learned much from it, it was an objective process. Still more objective was my approach to philosophers like Kant and Leibniz. The first reading of Kant's *Prologomena* was a revelation. I had never conceived that the process of abstract thought could be such a pure pleasure, and I seemed to become conscious for the first time of the beautiful functioning of an instrument which is the human brain. Rather different, but still impersonal, is the relationship which I have had with such philosophers as Bergson and Whitehead. In so far as I have myself indulged in any practical philosophy—it has been almost exclusively in the field of aesthetics—I have been strongly influenced by both these writers, but I have never shared their general outlook. This would apply to many other modern philosophers of whose thought traces might be found in my own writings— William James, Benedetto Croce, Leone Vivante, Max Scheler.

Of philosophers of the other kind, in whom I have found a sympathy which is emotional rather than intellectual, it occurs to me to mention only three: Traherne, Kierkegaard and Santayana. It is an odd and apparently disparate trinity, and it would be difficult to trace any lines of communication between them, or to give them a place in any orderly scheme of philosophical development. They just 'happened' to me, and it is a curious and disconcerting fact that I have remained in stubborn disagreement with the conclusions of two of them. They have been rather in the nature of friends whose faults I have seen, whose religious views I have ignored, but whom I have nevertheless loved and frequented because from them I derived the greatest pleasure and profit. Santayana comes first in time. I cannot remember when I first came across one of his books—I may have been led to him by William James, or perhaps it was his Introduction to the volume of Spinoza in the Everyman Library (first published as long ago as 1910) which aroused my curiosity. I also find it difficult to explain the fascination he has exercised on me for many years. I suppose it was partly the fact that here was a modern philosopher with the superficial appeal of a literary style—though the same was true of others, Bergson and Bradley, for example. Santayana's style has limitations, which I have discussed elsewhere; and in spite of his seductive charm, his prose is not easy to read at length. There was undoubtedly some more practical reason, and I can only suggest now that I hoped to find in him a philosophy which would reconcile our knowledge of the physical universe with some recognition of spiritual values. I never had much use for idealistic philosophy; I was a materialist, but for my materialism I wanted a philosophical, though not necessarily a metaphysical, sanction. 'Now in natural philosophy,' Santayana has said, 'I am a decided materialist—apparently the only one living; I am well aware that idealists are fond of calling materialism, too, metaphysics, in rather an angry tone, so as to cast discredit upon it by assimilating it to their own systems. But my materialism, for all that, is not metaphysical. . . . I wait for the men of science to tell me what matter is, in so far as they can discover it, and am not at all surprised or troubled at the abstractness and vagueness of their ultimate conceptions: how should our notion of things so remote from the scale and scope of our senses be anything *but schematic*?'* This has been my own attitude—a materialism which is not so much a part of my philosophy, as an external limitation, marking its boundaries. Though I still read meta-

* *Scepticism and Animal Faith*, pp. vii–viii.

physics when it comes my way or suits my mood, I have
been prevented from becoming a metaphysician by a strong
feeling that anything not evident to our senses, or to the
extension of our senses provided by scientific instruments,
is not of great importance to our lives. Even scientific speculations cease to interest me when they can only be handled
by means of mathematical symbols. If I cling to a realm
of supermaterial values, which Santayana calls the realm
of essence, it is because the existence of such values is as
evident to my senses as sticks or stones. For a knowledge
of the reality of these values I do not need to go further
than the realm of aesthetics. The poetic essence, for example, cannot be measured by any scientific instruments:
it is available to intuition alone, and the poetic data which
are given by intuition belong to a world as real as that
from which scientific observation draws its data. Whether
poetic data belong to the same order of existence as physical
data—whether, that is to say, there is any relationship between the world of matter and the world of values—this is
the kind of problem that Santayana discusses with such
acuity; and it is because he discusses such problems in
relation to human life rather than to a logical system that
I have always been drawn to his writings. 'The hierarchy
of goods, the architecture of values, is the subject that con-
cerns man most. Wisdom is the first philosophy, both in
time and authority; and to collect facts and chop logic
would be idle and would add no dignity to the mind, unless
that mind possessed a clear humanity and could discern
what facts and logic are good for and what not.' * In re-

* *Reason in Science,* p. 217.

nouncing metaphysics it was under Santayana's guidance that I became what must, I suppose, be called a moralist.

My attraction to Traherne is still more difficult to explain. *Centuries of Meditations* is in purpose a manual of devotion, far removed from my practices and beliefs. It is not as such that it has attracted me. 'There are invisible ways of conveyance by which some great thing doth touch our souls, and by which we tend to it,' says Traherne himself. It is some such invisible communication that runs between this book and me. There is, of course, the purely external and visible quality of the prose style, to which full justice has not even yet been done. Of his period, only Jeremy Taylor and Milton come into comparison, and though Traherne lacks the sustained eloquence of the one and the grandeur of the other, he has his own incomparable felicity. His lyrical spirituality, though it has a parallel in the contemporary poetry of Vaughan and Crashaw, is quite unique in English prose. But nevertheless it is not for its style alone that I have returned again and again to this book. It is for its content. 'An empty book,' Traherne begins, 'is like an Infant's Soul, in which anything may be written. It is capable of all things, but containeth nothing. I have a mind to fill this with profitable wonders. And since Love made you put it into my hands, I will fill it with those truths you love without knowing them: and with those things which, if it be possible, shall show my Love; to you, in communicating most enriching Truths: to Truth, in exalting her beauties in such a Soul.' It is an intimate induction, intended for the eyes of a friend, and it immediately puts the reader in the place of that friend. It gives us the key to the understanding of the book which follows. That there are Truths we love without knowing them must be the experience of everyone who finds that his actions are guided by a principle which finds no expression in his declared philosophy of life. This principle the Christian mystics have identified with Love— a universal love analogous to human love. And it is this love, in all its aspects, that Traherne describes. 'Love is deeper than at first it can be thought. It never ceaseth but in endless things.' It is an expansive love which gradually illuminates the whole universe and everything in it. 'Till your spirit filleth the whole world, and the stars are your jewels; till you are as familiar with the ways of God in all Ages as with your walk and table: till you are intimately ac- quainted with that shady nothing out of which the world was made: till you love men so as to desire their happiness, with a thirst equal to the zeal of your own; till you delight in God for being good to all: you never enjoy the world.' Traherne's religion is positive and joyful, far removed from the gloomy doctrines of predestination and original sin which had triumphed in his own life-time (he died in 1674). His mysticism is an affirmation of sensuous enjoyment—'by the very right of your senses you enjoy the world. . . . It is of the nobility of man's soul that he is insatiable.' The senses are God's instruments, and we minister to his power and goodness with these divine engines. We thus acquire a sense of the glory which is immanent in the world, and which we live to exploit, like veins of gold in the dull ore of experience. It is a pantheistic doctrine, since it holds that we only attain true happiness when we actively participate in the processes of nature.

THE FALCON AND THE DOVE

Traherne more than any other writer—more than the Golden Legend or the chronicles of the Middle Ages, more than Plutarch or Vauvenargues, William Blake or Henry James—all recognizable tributaries—confirmed me in that sense of glory which from my early youth I have identified with the source of all virtuous and unselfish actions. I have given this title, *The Sense of Glory,* to a collection of essays which help to define, however obliquely, what I mean by the phrase. But the truest and deepest meaning, of which my meaning is only a dim reflection, will be found in Traherne's *Centuries.* 'I will not by the noise of bloody wars and the dethroning of kings advance you to glory: but by the gentle ways of peace and love.' But the gentle ways are the ways of ecstasy: and ecstasy that comes from perceiving bright perfection in natural things, felicity in natural feelings, and celestial joy on your own threshold:

> But little did the infant dream
> That all the treasures of the World were by,
>   And that himself was so the cream
> And crown of all which around about did lie.
>   Yes thus it was! The gem,
>   The diadem,
>   The ring enclosing all
> That stood upon this earthly ball;
>   The heav'nly eye,
>   Much wider than the sky,
> Wherein they all included were,
> The glorious soul that was the king
> Made to possess them, did appear
>   A small and little thing!

Between Traherne and Kierkegaard there are, again, no visible communications. But when I read such a sentence of Traherne's as: 'To think well is to serve God in the interior court,' then I am reminded of Kierkegaard. Kierkegaard is much the latest of these three influences. From time to time I had noticed his name in connection with German philosophy, and more rarely he was referred to by French writers. But it was not until about 1930 that I began to search for his own works, in German or French translations (it is only recently that English translations have begun to appear). The revival of interest in Kierkegaard has been due largely to theologians, both Catholic and Protestant, and it is not possible to separate Kierkegaard's theological ideas from the rest of his work. Nevertheless, it is for his psychological and aesthetic implications that I have read him. He is the very incarnation of the principle of Negative Capability: the mythical Hamlet become flesh, in Hamlet's own haunt. His long search for a principle of true inwardness, for 'something which grows together with the deepest roots of my life, through which I am, so to speak, grafted upon the divine'—in this I found a new justification for my doctrine of the personality as opposed to the character. 'It is with joy,' writes Kierkegaard in his *Journals,* 'and inwardly strengthened, that I contemplate those great men who have thus found the precious stone, for the sake of which they sell all, even their lives, whether I see them intervene forcefully in life, and without faltering go forward on the path marked out for them, or discover them remote from the highway, absorbed in themselves and in working for their noble aim. And I look with reverence even upon the errors which lie so near by. It is this divine side of man, his inward action which means everything, not a mass of information; for that will certainly follow and then all that knowledge will not be a chance assemblage, or a succession of details, without system and without a focusing point. I too have certainly looked for such a center.' * Kierkegaard was essentially a poet, a child of the Romantic Movement; and he analyses every aspect of life with profundity, with irony, and often with lyrical feeling. His *Journals* have been compared with the *Confessions* of St. Augustine, the *Pensées* of Pascal, and the *Apologia* of Newman; they have something of the quality of all these great books, but they have something more— something nearer to Nietzsche than to anything suggested by these other names. In Kierkegaard, in fact, I was picking up the Nietzschean threads which I had let fall some ten years earlier. Kierkegaard belongs to an earlier age, and there is no evidence that Nietzsche was influenced by him. But many critics have been struck by the resemblance between these two great thinkers—a resemblance which has nothing to do with the content of their thought, but is rather due to the identical nature of their spiritual unrest—that unrest 'which goads the thinking spirit of man to go forth, beyond everything known, and to seek after the peace for which, without doubt, he longs.' †

We might say that there was the possibility of Nietszche in Kierkegaard, but that it was a possibility he deliberately

* *Journals,* translated by Alexander Dru. (Oxford, 1938), pp. 16–17.

† *Soren Kierkegaard,* by Theodor Haecker. Translated by Alexander Dru. (Oxford, 1937.)

rejected. Kierkegaard realized that the thinking spirit could only find peace in some firm anchorage. 'In order to sew one must knot the thread' was the metaphor he used; and he argued that there were three—and only three—such knots to tie in the otherwise unending process of dialectical reasoning. One is materialism—the world of observed and measured facts; a world of thought limited by our perceptions, but nevertheless a possible world to rest in. The second knot is aesthetics, which Kierkegaard, like Plato, recognized as the world of pure form—'form seeking and symbolizing the austere peace of eternity' (Haecker). The third knot is revelation, 'where dogma for both thought and thinker is the embodiment of the spirit, will, and word of God' (Haecker). Kierkegaard himself chose this third knot: he found that only a belief in the Christian myth could save him from despair; the aesthetic life in particular, he held, led to despair. One of his greatest books, *Enten/Eller* (*Either/Or*), is devoted to this dilemma: either the aesthetic life—or the ethical. That the aesthetic was for him, not merely a philosophical category, but a deep and real experience, is proved by his enthusiasm for the music of Mozart—not merely by the enthusiasm as such, but by the fact that the enthusiasm was precisely for Mozart, one of the most absolute artists that ever lived. 'Immortal Mozart! Thou to whom I owe all, to whom I owe it *that I lost my reason,* that my soul was in a maze, that I was dismayed in my inmost being. Thou to whom I owe it that I did not go through life without anything occurring that was capable of perturbing me deeply. Thou to whom I give thanks that I did not die without having loved, even though my love was an unhappy one.' That is the tribute of a man who has experienced the aesthetic act, not as reflection but as immediacy. The erotic immediacy which he found in the music of Mozart, and whose potentiality existed in himself as a poet, was something far too actual to be dismissed, in the manner of the philistine philosophers, as insignificant. It was, properly understood, a principle of life itself—a principle which Kierkegaard rejected, but which I, in all humility, have accepted. I am not confident enough to assert that in my case it can never entail the despair which Kierkegaard thought inevitable; but I do suggest that the principle was insufficient for Kierkegaard, and productive of despair, for personal reasons. 'Doubt is despair of thought, despair is doubt of the personality.' Darkening the whole of Kierkegaard's life is a sense of doom and retribution, an acceptance of death as a happy release from fear. The aesthetic principle is, however, an affirmation of life—of life as a sensuous end-in-itself, with spirituality satisfied in the contemplation of pure form. But this eudemonism has its mysticism: the immediacy of the aesthetic act, the sheer leap of genius into the freedom of creativity—that event which many great artists have described. Eudemonism is not a limited or shallow ethic; as Kierkegaard realized, it is a complete alternative to the religious ethic, and the only question is its subjective adequacy. But there is an insolence in the very attempt to formulate absolute values, for an individual can only contemplate his particular aspect of the universe. If he is wise he will not insist on the exclusiveness of any aspect; for just as he cannot stand in two places at one and the same time, so he cannot see the universe from more than one aspect: *either* one *or* the other.

THE TREE OF LIFE

Standing at the aesthetic point, Kierkegaard saw before him an abyss of despair. For myself, I can only say that standing at this same point I feel secure and happy.

It would take me too far from my immediate purpose to expound the aesthetic philosophy of life in any detail. Like religious philosophy, it has a rational justification: a philosophy of pure form derived, ultimately, from the physical laws of the universe, the laws which determine, not only the movement of planets and stars and the coherence of the structure of matter, but also the growth of organic life. But like religious philosophy, it cannot be included within such a rational framework: there is a limit to rationality, an 'instant' in which the spirit leaps out of the logical framework of thought, and is creative. What we call classical art is satisfied with the laws of universal beauty: harmony, balance and proportion. But what we call romantic art passes beyond these laws and proclaims its freedom, its novelty, its uniqueness. This act of freedom cannot be justified logically, any more than can an act of faith. It is an intuition, not merely of form and its plastic expression, but also of the paradox of a particular individual, a particular personality.

I shall be accused of reading my own views into the philosophy of Kierkegaard, but in justification I would like to quote a paragraph which Kierkegaard inserts into his eulogy of Mozart (in *Either/Or*). The paragraph is obscure if it is simply detached; what I give, therefore, is a paraphrase.* I have taken only one liberty: the obscurity of the paragraph is partly due, especially in an English translation, to the use

* Based on the translation given by Dr. Walter Lowrie in his *Kierkegaard* (Oxford, 1938).

of impersonal pronouns; what the pronouns stand for is obvious from the context—on the one hand they denote the 'erotic immediacy' of the aesthetic experience; on the other hand, Kierkegaard himself, or the poet who renounces the aesthetic experience. I have therefore ventured to actualize the passage: it is simple to use the personal pronoun for the poet, but to personify the forces latent in the aesthetic experience I have taken the 'angelic host' of Rilke's *Duinese Elegies.* This may seem a bold and unauthorized procedure, but I am convinced that what Kierkegaard and Rilke are writing about is an identical experience. Kierkegaard's paragraph would then read:

> The angelic host I have loved,
>   with whom I have lived fervently
>   all my youthful years,
> the voices that have whispered to me secretly—
>
>   Shyly I approach them
>   my feelings mingled and confused
>   because of the questioning purpose in my mind.
>
> Little by little I have learned to speak their tongue,
>   gathering their accents as a bird gathers wisps of straw,
>   more joyful over each scrap and fragment
>   than over all the rest of the world.
> My loving ear has listened to them in solitude,
>   alone in the great crowd,
>   unnoticed in my secret hiding-place.
> My greedy insatiable ear has sucked in their music,
> my avaricious ear has jealously treasured their songs,
>   never feeling secure;

my sleepless ear, ever attentive, has caught their softest
  resonance.

Theirs are the voices I have lived with by day,
theirs the voices I have heard in the night,
voices that have banished sleep and made me restless,
voices that have haunted my dreams,
voices I have wakened to, only to dream of again awake,
voices that have made me spring up in the night
  lest I should forget their message.

Such is the angelic host that appeared before me in my
  ecstasy.
They have followed me in the bright moonlit nights
  and to the solitary forests by the sea;
they have walked by my side in the dark streets
  at midnight and at break of day;
they have raced by my side on horseback,
they have accompanied me in my carriage,
they have filled my house with their presence,
they have penetrated into my own room.
Their voices have sounded in my ear
  and resounded in my soul:
the tissue of my soul is spun from their delicate strains.

—And now, like fabulous creatures from the sea
that rise with the seaweed clinging to their limbs,
these angels invade my reasoning mind
rise up out of the sea of recollection
  clothed with memories.

My soul is full of sorrow
  and my heart is tender,

for now I must say farewell to the angelic host.
We are parting
   never to meet again in time or eternity.

I am full of fear
as though I had broken a most solemn vow.
I am no longer the same,
   no longer young,
   no longer like a child.
I am afraid because I have lost the angelic voices
   that made me happy and joyful;
I am afraid lest the voices themselves should falter and
   hesitate
   unable to answer
   the questions which throng to my mind.

Alas, alas! all is lost.
The angels vanish
   nevermore to answer my call.

Kierkegaard realized—was perhaps the first philosopher to realize—that there exists between reason and inspiration exactly the same unbridgeable chasm as between reason and faith. Art, like dialectics, can proceed a certain distance with the aid of measurable quantities—the quantities of rhythm and harmony, for example; but there comes a point at which the creative spirit must leap into the unknown. It is at this point that romantic art begins. I do not imply that there is any relationship between romantic art and religion; indeed, what I have implied is that they are totally distinct aspects of the universe. But the relationship of the creative artist to his art is analogous to that between the believer and his faith.

THE TREE OF LIFE

Art is not in any sense a substitute for religion: the choice is between aesthetics and ethics. But just as ethics tends to seek the sanction of religious ritual and dogma, so aesthetics becomes existential and self-sufficient in the work of art. The aesthetic view of life is not, however, confined to those who can create or appreciate works of art. It exists wherever natural senses play freely on the manifold phenomena of our world, and where life as a consequence is found to be full of felicity. The problem is to preserve the naturalness of the senses—to avoid their distortion by the strains introduced into society by economic scarcity; to avoid their dissolution in systems of abstract thought; to avoid their defamation by the gloomy myths of those who fear death and turn against the bright manifestations of our earthly existence. In the past the equilibrium of society has been dependent on chance factors of climate and military power; but there is a prospect that in some not very distant future an equilibrium may be established by the reason and skill of a fully-conscious humanity. If that day comes, then the sense of glory which has only made intermittent appearances in our history will pervade the whole realm of existence. This does not mean that we shall escape the tragic sense of life which comes when we accept death as inevitable, arbitrary, and final. Only those who have experienced the anguish and sorrow at the base of human existence are brave enough to seek to transfigure its brief span.

4

THE EARTHLY PARADISE

E NGLISH farmers are a conservative class. Whether they are yeoman farmers owning their own land or tenant farmers renting it from a landlord, they tend to identify their interests with the land-owning aristocracy. They never seem to question the right of the landlord to a tax which often amounts to several hundred pounds annually and which must be paid not for the enjoyment of a property, but for the right to cultivate it. Such cultivation, without which the land would go to waste, is due to the skill of the farmer and the physical energy of the farm-laborer—the hardest worker in the country and the worst paid. The farmer is, in fact, the buffer between the landlord and the laborer. In many cases he is little more than an agent or bailiff, farming the land for the benefit of the landlord, and dependent on that landlord for the upkeep of his capital goods—his barns and stables, his roads and fences. Corresponding to this economic bond is a social bond: the farmer likes to think of himself as on the fringes of the landed aristocracy. He subscribes to the local hunt, hunts with the gentry as a social equal, and at such functions as the annual hunt-ball associates even more intimately with them. The local Conservative Party is merely an extension of this social chain: it would be a queer sort of farmer that identified himself with the local Labour Party, and therefore with the political outlook of his laborers. In my father's time there was no Labour Party, but the Liberal Party was in this respect little better. If it did not openly solicit the laborer's vote, it leaned to that side of the social scale. More fundamentally, by its policy of free trade it was the party of those commercial and industrial interests that were willing to sacrifice England's agriculture for the sake of a general expansion of trade.

By tradition and almost by instinct, therefore, I at first adopted the politics of the Conservative Party. From the age of fifteen I began to take a serious interest in the subject, and as I have already related, I absorbed, not only the propaganda of the party, but even its historical and philosophical background. I remember that I almost learned by heart a small book on *Conservatism* which Lord Hugh Cecil wrote at this time. My appreciation of Burke and Bolingbroke must have been superficial; but Disraeli was another question. He was the first author that I read systematically—I read his novels one by one until I had exhausted them, and I studied all the published material about his life. This infatuation was, of course, significant. Disraeli is a romantic figure, and his writings are romances in the strict meaning of that word. But he wrote no romance half so entrancing as his own life. That this obscure Jewish boy should rise, by virtue of his talents alone, to become the leader of the British aristocracy, the Prime Minister and favorite confidant of the Queen, and, more fantastic still, the statesman who first made the British Empire a conscious unity on the Roman model—this is one of the strangest stories in history. It is strange to the point of being grotesque, and its very possibility is perhaps a crystallization of the paradox which lies at the heart of an empire like ours. For empires are not planned: they are the gradual actualization of a myth: as splendid, as formless and as impermanent as the clouds which gather in an April sky.

I think it is conceivable that Disraeli, with his two nations of the rich and the poor, planted the first seeds of doubt in my conservative mind. But in Toryism—which word, in spite of Peel's intention, represents something more fundamental and philosophical than Conservatism—there is an ethical strain which easily gives birth to a social conscience. It has often been remarked that many of the greatest social reforms have been carried out by the Tory Party. To some extent this is a reaping of the harvest which other parties have sown; but it is also due to a sense of responsibility, last remnant of the feudal tradition, and to that rare form of patriotism which puts the welfare of the nation before the interests of the commercial classes. The distinction between Town and Country, the City and the Land, upon which the old two-party system was really based, has been largely obliterated; but one still finds conservatives who are not to be identified with Capital and who have a far wider and more generous outlook than many who profess to represent the poor and oppressed.

The fundamental contrasts between town and country, industry and agriculture, wealth and poverty, were forced upon me by my daily experiences in Leeds. Up to the age of fifteen I had no knowledge of town life; for the next six years I was to see little else. For three years, with only one week's break in the year, I walked these streets—I could not afford a tram fare. From my home on the outskirts to the Bank in the middle of the city; from the head-office of the Bank to the branches at Armley, Beeston and Chapeltown, I passed through areas in which factories were only relieved by slums, slums by factories—a wilderness of stone and brick, with soot falling like black snow. Drab and stunted wage-slaves drifted through the stink and clatter; tramcars moaned and screeched along their glistening rails, spluttering blue electric sparks. These same wage-slaves brought their savings to the Bank—we accepted deposits of three-pence and upwards—greasy coins which blackened the fingers that counted them, and were then entered into pass-books permeated by grime and sweat. For a year or two my way home passed through the City Square, where a political agitator sometimes drew a crowd round him; and sometimes I would stop and listen. In one way or another, this environment gradually penetrated the armor of my inherited prejudices. Ugliness and poverty, dirt and drabness, were too universal to be ignored. The questioning intelligence which was slowly awakening in me began to question the material things before my eyes. I found that other people had questioned them: not only Disraeli, but Carlyle, Ruskin and Morris; and that they were being questioned by people round about me.

Plato has written about the windows that open into the mind, and it is a very true image. The mind of youth is a room without an escape: there is perhaps a dim inner light, and an endless succession of pictures flicker on the walls. Then suddenly, on one side, the shutters are drawn and through an open space the youth looks out onto the light and landscape of the real world. Some time after, another window is opened, and the world is seen from another aspect. The process should continue until there are windows open on every side of the mind, and the whole universe is visible to the inquiring eye.

This sudden awakening to the nature of my social environment was indeed like a new window opening onto the world: a window through which I not only saw the social realities, but by whose light I also read what had been written about them. Again I read eagerly and indiscriminately—chiefly Carlyle, Ruskin and Morris, but also a mass of propagandist literature, periodicals like Blatchford's *Clarion,* Fabian tracts, obscure pamphlets of all kinds. Later, in my second year at the University, and until I left for the Army, I was to study these questions more systematically: I read the classical economists under D. H. Macgregor and Henry Clay, social economics and economic history under Arthur Greenwood. Indeed, economics is the one subject in which I have possibly had what pedagogues would call a 'thorough grounding.' It is a subject of which I have made least use in life.

This 'thorough grounding' did not, of course, include anything so unorthodox as Karl Marx and Bakunin; but all the same I was inevitably drawn to these two opposed forces in the socialist movement. I still possess the copy of the Sonnenschein edition of *Capital* which I bought at this time, and its well-scored pages indicate with what care I studied the whole volume. On the other side I was much influenced by Kropotkin's *Fields, Factories and Workshops,* and by his pamphlets on *Anarchist Morality* and *Anarchist Communism* (published by the Freedom Press in 1912 and 1913). A pamphlet by Edward Carpenter on *Non-Governmental Society* (1911) was even more decisive, and I find tucked into the copy which, like my Marx, has survived all these years, the following 'statement' of my own views:

As I believe that the society outlined in this pamphlet is an ideal not immediately realizable, I should like to sketch out the path along which I think society will evolve.

There are two distinct types of modern socialism: Collectivism, which looks at things solely from the consumer's point of view; and Syndicalism, which looks at things solely from the producer's point of view. Both are fundamentally wrong: society must be regarded as an entity—a co-ordination of consumer and producer. But these two forces, acting in opposite directions, will produce, as though by a parallelogram of forces, a resultant force which will be the true Socialism, combining the good of both Collectivism and Syndicalism. For the present, both Collectivism and Syndicalism have their respective duties. The role of Collectivism is the expropriation of Capital. This is to be brought about by the nationalization of industry. But Collectivists are wrong in regarding nationalization as an end in itself: it is only a means. For whilst the Collectivist state is evolving, Syndicalism will be playing its role—i.e., it will be developing the economic, industrial and educational functions of the Trade Unions. Trade Unions are, I am convinced, the units upon which the future society will be built. They must be organized and extended so as to be powerful enough to demand, and fit enough to undertake, the control of industry when it has been nationalized by the state. When we have traveled so far, society will be capable of evolving into the ideal state suggested by this pamphlet. By a devolution of power, a decentralization of control, and, above all, by a development in the social conscience of the nation, the ideals of today will become the realities of tomorrow.

And morality, which has always evolved parallel to the economic evolution of society, will change with these changes. The perfect morality is only possible in the perfect society.

The true social faith is, I think, to work for the immediate practical objects of socialism, but at the same time to keep before us always some ultimate ideal—some goal to which we may aim.

This cannot have been written later than the summer of 1914, and it might be as much as a year earlier. In the thirty odd years which have since elapsed, my political opinions have varied considerably (though always within the broad basic principles of socialism). What surprises me now, in 1946, is to find that the views I expressed at the age of twenty are the views I still hold. I should not now express them so naïvely; and the evolution of the Trade Unions since 1914 has brought them to a condition of bureaucratic conservatism hardly compatible with the role ascribed to them in my statement. It must also be confessed that syndicalism, both as a name and as a movement, has not in this country become the established force that seemed imminent in 1914. But whether we call it syndicalism or not, a movement that will look forward to the organization of the Trade Unions as units of production is essential equally to the collectivist and the anarchist form of socialism. The fundamental difference between anarchism and collectivism does not concern the economic function of the Trade Unions, but rather their relation to the state, and generally the distribution of power or authority between the center and the periphery of the economic sphere.

Anarchism was to suffer an almost complete eclipse in this country after the war. Kropotkin returned to Russia and died there in 1921, disillusioned and rejected. The intellectuals who in this country might have given their support to the movement were drawn away to the alternative of Guild Socialism, then being advocated with great fervor by A. R. Orage in the *New Age*. I myself became a sympathetic supporter of this new policy, and contributed at least two articles to the official organ of the group, the *Guildsman*, then edited by G. D. H. Cole. But meanwhile another influence intervened—Georges Sorel. His *Reflections on Violence* was published in a translation by T. E. Hulme in 1916, when I immediately acquired it. Few books have impressed me so deeply and so permanently. It worked on me in a surer way than Nietzsche had done. It appealed to something more fundamental than my intellect—namely, to my temperament and instincts—and again opened up endless new perspectives. It was from Sorel, if I remember rightly, that I passed to Bergson, and certainly to Proudhon. But his main function, in my case, was to supply to socialism the imaginative qualities which I found lacking in Marx. It is true that there were implications in Sorel which I did not then grasp, and which in the years to come were to lead in the direction of fascism rather than of socialism; and I only swallowed his doctrine of classicism because it seemed to me to be more romantic than romanticism itself—rather like Goethe's classicism. To expect a return of the classical spirit through the struggle of the classes; to maintain that only under the influence of the classical ideal could the working-class movement succeed in regenerating society— that, indeed, was more romantic than, say, Marx's General Law of Capitalist Accumulation.*

The proselytizing fervor with which I adopted Sorel's views is shown by a letter which I wrote to the *Yorkshire Post* on the appearance of a review of *Reflections on Violence,* and which they printed under my initials.

M. SOREL AND SYNDICALISM

To the Editor of the *Yorkshire Post.*

Sir,—Your reviewer of Sorel's *Reflections on Violence* fails to present your readers with the true import of that book. His interpretation of the role of proletarian violence is completely misleading, simply because he does not recognize that Sorel's theories are complementary and not complete. Sorel perfects a social philosophy; he does not posit one. His theory is nothing more than an amplification of Marx's hypothesis of a fatalistic revolution.

* It is significant that those critics who have been most influenced by Sorel's classicism and anti-humanism have tended to discard his revolutionary syndicalism, whilst those whose tendency has been to retain the syndicalism have discarded the classicism. Sorel's inconsistency is thus proved by the subsequent history of his ideas. If it is argued that a more perceptive intelligence would have been attracted to the superior consistency of Marx's theory of history, the reply would be that consistency in this case has proved no less fallible, and has been far more disastrous in its practical consequences.

THE EARTHLY PARADISE

You will remember, Sir, how Marx conceives a capitalist class progressing and concentrating; a proletariat, organizing; and a social revolution as a *coup d'état*.* Now it is vital to this hypothesis that the capitalist class should progress, distinct and powerful. If once it becomes intermingled with the proletariat; if once it surrenders a part of its power—then Marx's hypothesis is defeated. A successful revolution becomes impossible. Hence the syndicalist opposition to schemes of co-operation and social amelioration. Hence Sorel's concern for the vigor of the middle classes. Not, as your reviewer has it, because he wishes to preserve them as directors of the social organism, but because their progress is vital to revolution—because, when the revolution does come, he wishes the revolutionaries to inherit an economically vigorous society and not a slough of economic decadence. He sees the capitalist and the proletariat as the participants in a world tragedy—a tragedy having as its dénouement not the reformed society of the 'worthy progressive,' but a new society with new cultural values. But listen to Sorel himself:

'The dangers which threaten the future of the world may be avoided if the proletariat hold on with obstinacy to revolutionary ideas, so as to realize as much as possible Marx's conception. Everything may be saved if the proletariat, by their use of violence, manage to re-establish the division into classes, and so restore to the middle class something of its former energy; that is the great aim towards which the whole thought of men —who are not hypnotized by the event of the day, but think of the conditions of tomorrow—must be directed. Proletarian violence, carried on as a pure and simple manifestation of the

* As the editor of the *Yorkshire Post* pointed out in his reply, a *coup d'état* was not at all characteristic of Marx's conception of revolution.

143

class war, appears thus as a very fine and very heroic thing; it is at the service of the immemorial interests of civilization; it is perhaps not the most appropriate method of obtaining immediate material advantages, but it may save the world from barbarism.'

Now, perhaps, your reviewer will understand why Sorel regarded a great European war as an alternative to proletarian violence. It is because such a war tends to accentuate, in its after-effects, class differences. The resultant quickening of commercial interests will give to the middle classes new life and independence. The aftermath of poverty and disorganization of labor will inspire the proletariat with heroic and revolutionary spirit. Once more we shall have the social protagonists implacably opposed. And the premises of Marx's fatalistic hypothesis will be present and the conclusion duly fulfilled.

It is hopeless for anyone to attempt to understand or accept this new social doctrine unless he rid himself of every post-Renaissance humanistic prejudice in his thought. Syndicalism is not the babblings of a lot of ignorant workmen. It is the political equivalent of anti-Romanticism in literature. It is the social manifestation of anti-humanistic revolt—of a return to a classical and a pessimistic conception of the universe.—Yours, etc.

The last paragraph of this letter is a paraphrase of Hulme's Introduction to the translation of *Reflections on Violence*. I think now that there is more in it of Hulme than of Sorel, and certainly more of Hulme and Sorel than of my own views. I have no doubt that at the time I did genuinely profess anti-humanistic and anti-romantic opinions, but they were based on the historical ambiguity of these words. The confusion is due to Hulme rather than to Sorel;

Hulme's own ideas were in a state of flux at the time, as his collected papers (*Speculations*) which I was to edit after the war, sufficiently prove. Looking through Sorel's book now, I find nothing classical, in the normal sense of the word, in his conception of violence and revolution. His tragic conception of life, and his belief in absolute values, do indeed spring from his admiration of Greek drama. But the mistake is to assume that Greek drama is necessarily anti-humanistic or even anti-romantic. Neither a tragic conception of life nor absolute values are inconsistent with romantic art, as represented, for example, by Homer, Shakespeare or Blake. In the following passage from Sorel's book, which I marked with emphatic approval in 1916, there is latent the whole of my subsequent elaboration of a doctrine of romantic art:

Like industry, art has never adapted itself to the demands of theorists; it always upsets their plans of social harmony, and humanity has found the freedom of art far too satisfactory ever to think of allowing it to be controlled by the creators of dull systems of sociology. The Marxists are accustomed to seeing the ideologists look at things the wrong way round, and so, in contrast to their enemies, they should look upon art as a reality which begets ideas and not as an application of ideas.

It is precisely the academicians, the natural supporters of classicism, who attempt to make of art an instrument for the application of ideas (of *their* ideas, of course). Sorel was certainly not an academician; nor, in this sense, was he a classicist.

My political education continued actively during the war, and I occasionally gave expression to my opinions in the

New Age and elsewhere. But when, after the war, I entered the Civil Service, I found myself under a much stricter censorship, and though I never 'dropped' politics, I ceased to write about them. When in 1931 I left the Civil Service and was once more at liberty to take part in the public discussion of political issues, some people assumed that I had 'just discovered' Marx, that the turn of political events had forced me from the seclusion of an ivory tower, that I had adopted anarchism as a logical counterpart to my views on art. Actually there was an unfailing continuity in my political interests and political opinions. I would not like to claim that they show an unfailing consistency, but the general principles which I found congenial thirty years ago are still the basic principles of such political philosophy as I now accept.*

In calling these principles Anarchism I have forfeited any claim to be taken seriously as a politician, and have cut myself off from the main current of socialist activity in England. But I have often found sympathy and agreement in unexpected places, and there are many intellectuals who are fundamentally anarchist in their political outlook, but who do not dare to invite ridicule by confessing it. The word is, of course, nearly as ambiguous as 'classicism' and 'romanticism'; and like these words it indicates a general outlook, a Weltanschauung, rather than a practical program. Most people are content with practical issues: they think that if they plan the economy of the state for the immediate future by reconciling all conflicting interests, or by subordinating these interests to the general good, they have

* And have expressed in *Poetry and Anarchism* (Faber, 1938) and *The Politics of the Unpolitical* (Routledge, 1944).

done all that is necessary, or humanly possible. Their ethos, if they have one, is vaguely religious, and complacently traditional. They forget that you cannot move one step without moving in a specific direction; and that if you do not keep looking at a fixed point on the horizon, you walk in circles. Anarchism is a point on the horizon: it has no plan to be put into being tomorrow or the next day. It does not believe in plans, which are rational constructions that always leave out the imponderable and elusive factors of human feeling and human instinct. When Confucius complained to Lao Tzu that though he had tried to get seventy-two rulers to adopt his plans for the government of the state—his six scriptures—not one of them had any use for them, Lao Tzu replied: 'It is a lucky thing that you did not meet with a prince anxious to reform the world. Those six scriptures are the dim footprints of ancient kings. They tell us nothing of the force that guided their steps. All your lectures are concerned with things that are no better than footprints in the dust. Footprints are made by shoes; but they are far from being shoes.' *

Confucius was a conservative planner; but Lao Tzu would have said the same to a socialist planner. There is only one necessary plan—the plan of nature. We must live according to natural laws, and by virtue of the power which comes from concentrating upon their manifestation in the individual mind. Anarchism asserts—it is its only assertion—that life must be so ordered that the individual can live a natural life, 'attending to what is within.' But once you begin to

* From *Three Ways of Thought in Ancient China,* by Arthur Waley (London, 1939).

work out the implications of this principle, you do not end until you have abolished the state. For if people began to live by natural law, there would be no need for man-made laws, nor for a government to enforce such laws.

We agree, many people will say; but what about our immediate problems? What about poverty and unemployment; slums and malnutrition; aggression and war? These problems, I readily admit, must be solved. Let us solve them in the manner suggested by democratic socialism—that seems the fairest and most practical method, but only if we keep the anarchist principle in mind at every stage and in every act. Then we shall avoid the fatal mistakes which have been made in Russia. We shall avoid creating an independent bureaucracy, for that is another form of tyranny, and the individual has no chance of living according to natural laws under such a tyranny. We shall avoid the creation of industrial towns which separate men from the fields and from the calming influences of nature. We shall control the machine, so that it serves our natural needs without endangering our natural powers. Thus in a thousand ways the principle of anarchism will determine our practical policies, leading the human race gradually away from the state and its instruments of oppression towards an epoch of wisdom and joy.

5

THE IMPACT OF WAR

AT THE outbreak of war in 1914 I was already in a military camp. This was not the outcome of any immediate patriotic zeal on my part, but was to some extent a consequence of my patriotic past. A year or two before I became an undergraduate, and while still contemplating the possibility of a medical career, I had joined the local territorial unit of the Royal Army Medical Corps in the vain hope that I should acquire some practical experience. By the time I reached the University, this had become a meaningless and arduous engagement, to which I was nevertheless bound for a period of years. But at the University there was an Officers' Training Corps, and I eagerly seized the opportunity to transfer my military bond to this more agreeable branch of the service. It is true that as time went on and my political ideas developed in the manner just related, I had certain qualms of conscience. But very few of those who joined the O.T.C. in those days had any serious motive. War was considered as a very remote contingency, and meanwhile here was an open-air club, with possibilities of friendship and youthful enterprise, and an annual camp which was in effect a free holiday for many who could not otherwise afford one. I was not interested in sport of any kind, and the O.T.C. provided me with my one physical diversion. I enjoyed the game very much.

There, happily at play, I was caught by the war. In the years that followed I was often to ask myself what I would have done if I had been a free agent. Politically I was a pacifist, and regarded the war as a conflict between rival imperial powers which would bring destruction to the peoples engaged. I hoped that the war would be stopped by international working-class action, and the failure of the responsible leaders to bring about a stoppage was my first lesson in political disillusionment. But fundamentally—that is to say, ethically—I could not claim to be a pacifist. It must be remembered that in 1914 our conception of war was completely unreal. We had vague childish memories of the Boer War, and from these and from a general diffusion of Kiplingesque sentiments, we managed to infuse into war a decided element of adventurous romance. War still appealed to the imagination. To this romantic illusion must be added, in my own case, a state of uncertainty about my future. Though I was ambitious and full of determination, I had no precise career marked out: I was to be a free-lance of some sort, and a free-lance finds a very appropriate place in an army. The war meant a decision: a crystallization of vague projects: an immediate acceptance of the challenge of life. I did not hesitate.

I received a commission within six months and was posted to a battalion of the Green Howards, my local North Riding regiment, then training in Dorset. This battalion had, like most of the newly formed units, a nucleus of regular officers drawn from one of the first-line battalions, together with a few reservists, but the bulk of the officers were recruits from the O.T.C. It happened that a considerable group in my particular battalion came from Eton (including two masters, Young and Slater); and practically all the others were from public schools. I had, therefore, stumbled into a very select and at first very uncongenial coterie. It must be remembered that I had not hitherto been outside my provincial fastness; but it was not so much my rawness (concealed as it was by my natural diffidence) as my incredible naïveté which was at fault. I will give two examples. I had become a regular reader of the *New Age,* at that time the most independent and lively periodical being published. The officers' mess occupied a building ordinarily used by the local masonic lodge, and there we had an ante-room where all the usual magazines and newspapers were available. They were displayed on a green-baize table, and there, when I had read it, I left my copy of the *New Age.* I was seated deep in an armchair one afternoon when the senior subaltern, traditionally responsible for the social conduct of the junior subalterns, came up to the table and casually picked up the *New Age.* He looked at it for a minute or two and slowly the color deepened in his rather florid face. He turned suddenly to address the room, and holding the paper up between his finger and thumb as though it was unclean, he shouted in a loud voice: 'Who brought this bloody rag into the mess?' I wish I could say that I sprang to my feet to defend my intellectual interests; but alas, I was not so naïve as that. I shrank still deeper into my chair and watched the angry senior subaltern stalk out in disgust, throwing the offensive periodical into the waste-paper basket as he passed. I had learned my lesson, and in the future read the *New Age* in the privacy of my tent or cubicle.

The other incident was similar and occurred shortly afterwards. The mess was actually the only place where, that bitter winter, one could read in comfort—I was still under canvas. One Sunday afternoon I took down with me a book I had just bought—Butler's *Erewhon Revisited*—and was soon absorbed in it. The mess was, as I had anticipated, nearly empty, but presently Captain Slater, the Eton master already mentioned, came in and passing behind my chair, observed the title of my book. 'O God! O Montreal!', he cried, 'that I should find someone reading Sam Butler in the British Army.' He was genuinely amused and interested, and though we were too disparate in age and temperament ever to become close friends, a sympathetic bond did henceforth exist between us.

But that, too, was a lesson. So long as we remained in England I confined my mess reading to the *Tatler* and the *Bystander* and other periodicals of the kind which were the only literary recreations of the majority of His Majesty's officers. When we reached the Front the situation changed, in this as in many other respects.

Meanwhile I was reacting to a new and unexpected mode of life. For the first time I was compelled to be continuously active in the open air, and though the strain was great, there was exhilaration in meeting it. For the first time, again, I was thrown against all sorts and conditions of men: on the one side I had to adapt myself to the manners and habits of my fellow officers, most of whom came from an entirely different and wealthier social world; and on the other side I became personally responsible for a platoon of soldiers, the majority of them toughened in the mines and factories of Durham and North Yorkshire. I found the officers more difficult than the men. The colonel was comprehensible: he was an English gentleman of a type I had been familiar with in my childhood, a good soldier in wartime and a good squire in peacetime; and there were two or three other regulars who were at any rate efficient and experienced. But the majority—young subalterns fresh from Sandhurst and the public-school boys already mentioned, struck me as snobbish and intolerant, and as trying to import into the Army the prefectorial spirit which they had acquired at school. Luckily I was not alone outside this predominant group, and some half-a-dozen of us managed to make our own society; one of these remains a close friend to the present day.

This sense of disunity lasted during the training period in England. In France the pressure of events, particularly the test of danger, quickly changed the atmosphere. Social values yielded to realistic values. In England we had unconsciously accepted the habit of command and the air of superiority which environment and education had conferred on the sons of the elite. Now we discovered that something else mattered more: that irreducible element of personality which is the raw material of education and the principle of growth persisting through every environment. It is my conviction that education and environment cannot change this innate spirit of an individual. Education can adapt the individual to his environment: it can explain life and reality to him and thus enable him to face them more skillfully with the gifts with which he is naturally endowed. It can also make him more conscious of the scope or limitation of these gifts. In the same way war, which is so often made the melodramatic agent of changes in character, does not affect the inherent quality of the person. As the months went by, I was to see all the proud pretensions which men had acquired from a conventional environment sink into insignificance before the basic facts of body and spirit. In my own case I was to discover, with a sense of self-confidence wholly new to me, that I could endure the experience of war, even at its worst. This is far from claiming that I was fearless: the first days in the trenches, the first bombardment or attack, was a draining sickness of the spirit. But I presently recovered, as from a plunge into a cold sea. What I found most difficult to accustom myself to, even after months at the Front, was the sight of human blood, and the stiff horror of a human corpse. That one does eventually get used to such things does not necessarily mean a deadening of the sensibility; but when an experience is repeated often enough, one has to rationalize it—in other words, make one's philosophy fit the facts.

I do not intend to give a detailed account of the four and a half years I spent in the Army: it is the totality of the experience which has significance for my present purpose. But there are two incidents which I have related with some attempt at an analysis of my accompanying feelings while they were still fresh in my mind—a raid which took place in the early summer of 1917 and the retreat of the Fifth Army from St. Quentin in March, 1918. The first of these narratives was published in 1930 in a small collection of prose pieces which I called *Ambush;* the second was written in 1919, but first published by Leonard and Virginia Woolf at the Hogarth Press six years later.

These short narratives are reproduced as separate chapters in the following pages. To the best of my ability 'The Raid,' which does not deviate in the least degree from the truth, adequately represents for me the subjective experience of war. The raid itself was, of course, a comparatively intense moment in the general course of that experience, and there were long stretches of boredom and inaction which should no doubt be reckoned as part of the total impact. But in so far as fear is the core of that experience, and the phenomenon about which those who have not experienced war betray the most curiosity, the analysis given in this narrative is the only evidence I have to offer. Whether we reach the reality by analysis, which is a subjective instrument, is another question; but in so far as the events can speak for themselves, they do so in 'In Retreat,' which I have tried to make an objective record.

If I had entered the war in a certain spirit of adventurous acceptance, as it was prolonged year after year it began to conflict with the impatient spirit of youth. One week in the trenches was sufficient to strip war of its lingering traces of romance: there was nothing, in the Ypres Salient where I first went into the line, but primitive filth, lice, boredom and death. Even the novelty of the experience, in such circumstances, is no palliative. But after weeks, and then months, and finally years of such a life, with no moral sanction to support the spirit, no fervor or enthusiasm, no hatred of the enemy, the whole business became fantastically unreal, a monstrous nightmare from which one could not awake. It should be remembered that a modern army is largely made up of young civilians without political experience, and the propaganda which is designed to inspire them (and perhaps does inspire them for a time) soon wears thin against the crude realities of war. If only, I used to think, we poor bloody soldiers could walk out, walk home, and leave the politicians to make the best of a quarrel which we did not understand and which had no interest for us! But though these were the sentiments of nine men out of ten, there was no possibility of proceeding to action. A soldier is part of a machine: once the machine is in movement, he functions as part of that machine, or simply gets killed. There is very little scope for individual initiative, for non-cooperation. It is true that one need not—and I did not—industriously strive to kill. During the whole war I never deliberately or consciously killed an individual man, with the possible exception of the one who was accompanying the German officer in the raid I am going to describe. I fired in self-defense, at advancing masses of men; but I never in cold blood selected my mark, with the intention of bringing to an end a human life. In April, 1918, when on a daylight 'contact' patrol with two of my men, we suddenly confronted, round some mound or excavation, a German patrol of the same strength. We were perhaps twenty yards from each other, fully visible. I waved a weary hand, as if to say: What is the use of killing each other? The German officer seemed to understand, and both parties turned and made their way back to their own trenches. Reprehensible conduct, no doubt, but in April, 1918, the war-weariness of the infantry was stronger than its pugnacity, on both sides of the line.

The impact of war on my sensibility is best revealed in the change which came to my writing during the period. As I have already said, it was a change of content rather than of technique. In 1915 I was already writing in the imagist manner, and from the Front I sent to the *Gryphon,* the student's magazine at Leeds, various contributions of which the earliest must have been written within a few weeks of my war experience. They are, as imagist poems should be, coldly objective. The following is an impression of Ypres:

> With a chill and hazy light
>   the sun of a winter noon
>   swills
>   thy ruins.
>
> Thy ruins etched
>   in silver silhouettes
>   against a turquoise sky.
>
> Lank poles leap to the infinite,
>   their broken wires
>   tossed like the rat-locks of Maenades.
>
> And Desolation broods over all,
>   gathering to her lap
>   her leprous children.
>
> The sparrows whimper
>   amid the broken arches.

Besides these poems, some short prose sketches in a 'Zarathustran' style called 'Fables from Flanders,' were published during 1916. They are still very idealistic, but a realistic note is creeping in, and towards the end of 1916 I find two poems which I called 'Truth for a Change—an Epilogue to the Fables.' In 1919 I apparently thought they were too sentimental to be included in *Naked Warriors,* but I reproduce one of them now as a contrast to the poem already quoted:

Such a lad as Harry was
Isn't met with every day.
He walked the land like a god,
Exulting in energy,
Care-free,
His eyes a blue smile
Beneath his yellow curling locks;
And you'd wonder where a common laborer got
Those deep Rossetti lips
And finely carven nose. . . .
I saw him stretch his arms
Languid as a dozing panther,
His face full to the clean sky—
When a blasted sniper laid him low:
He fell limp on the muddy boards
And left us all blaspheming.

I do not suggest that from a literary point of view such relatively crude and sentimental realism is an improvement on the earlier idealism: indeed, if there is any difference of merit, I am inclined to think that the Ypres poem is better than 'Truth for a Change.' But I should not have thought so in 1916—much less so in 1917 or 1918. My experience, that is to say, was modifying my literary values, and not altogether for the good. It is still a common assumption—Mr. Desmond MacCarthy made it only yesterday (14th January, 1940) in the *Sunday Times*—that generous feelings and humane sentiments are more important in poetry than what Mr. MacCarthy calls 'tessellating together unexpected words.' It depends on what Mr. MacCarthy means by his derogatory phrase; but in fact poetry is made with words, and cannot be made without a fine sense of the right words. Can Mr. MacCarthy discover much 'thought and feeling' in 'Kubla Khan'? Poetry, it would seem from this supreme example, can get along with a minimum of sentiment, provided it has a sufficiency of sensibility. But this is not to deny that good poetry can be made out of emotional situations, and in so far as the war induced me to write about emotional situations, it meant an enlargement of my literary experience. But it does not need a war to effect that change in a poet: I should have been brought to it by the impact of life itself.

The war did, of course, broaden in an altogether unexpected fashion my human contacts—far more than any school or university could have done. As the war developed, I found in my fellow officers a rough equivalent of the society of a university, but more diverse, and deepened and concentrated by the common sharing of dangerous purposes. I had such friends then as I had never had before or since—friends with whom one lived in a complete communal bond of thoughts as well as goods. When peace came, and the bond was destroyed, we drifted apart, back to the alien ways of our different social levels, our different environments and careers. Perhaps most significantly, we lost our masculine exclusiveness.

The most broadening of contacts was, however, that with the rank and file. I can only speak for the infantry, and I only speak of the infantry at war, away from the barracks and parade ground. Then between the company officer and his men there is every opportunity for the development of a relationship which abolishes all class distinctions and which can have a depth of understanding and sympathy for which I know no parallel in civilian life. Unfortunately the word 'leader' now belongs to the ideology of fascism, and in its blustering, commanding sense it was never applicable to a boyish officer in his early twenties, in charge of sixty or more men, many of whom would be much older and more experienced (now it may be different for there is more uniformity of age in a conscript army). The relationship was much more like that of a priest to his parish: for the company officer was the medium of communication with higher authority, one who interpreted the orders and strategy laid down by that authority, one who was therefore the ear and the voice of his group. Within the group he was responsible for the material welfare and comfort of his men—their food and billets, their health, their correspondence, and he it was who communicated with their relatives in case of death. In the trenches a platoon officer would often be isolated for many days with his men, and away from the rest of the officers; his closest companions were at all times his sergeant, his batman and his runner. It was only the social misfit, the public-school snob or the worse snob who came from the fringes of the working-classes, who could not develop a relationship of trust and even of intimacy with his men:

During the war I used to feel that this comradeship which had developed among us would lead to some new social order when peace came. I used to imagine an international party of ex-combatants, united by their common suffering, who would turn against the politicians and the profiteers in every country, and create a society based on respect for the individual human being. But no such party came into existence. The war ended in despair in Germany, in silly jubilation in England, and in an ineffective spirit of retribution in France. The societies of ex-combatants that were formed in England devoted themselves either to jingo heartiness or to the organization of charitable benefits. We left the war as we entered it: dazed, indifferent, incapable of any creative action. We had acquired only one new quality: exhaustion.

I shall relate in a later chapter the stages by which I re-adapted myself to civilian life. Here I only wish to describe the immediate reaction and disillusionment. My political ideas had continued to develop during the war. I published articles on syndicalism and guild socialism in 1917 and 1918. But the political situation of 1919 offered no basis for allegiance or enthusiasm. The political parties were all in the hands of non-combatants, especially on the left; and deep within me was a feeling that I could not speak the language of such people, must less cooperate with them. It was not that I despised them: I even envied them. But between us was a dark screen of horror and violation: the knowledge of the reality of war. Across that screen I could not communicate. Nor could any of my friends who had had the same experience. We could only stand on one side, like exiles in a strange country. Twenty-six years have passed and we have experienced another war. My feelings have not changed. I have seen the men of another generation engaged in a similar enterprise. Perhaps they have been less confident than we were, less liable to be deceived; but we do not know —they were conscripts and as such their motives were enigmatic. And since it was not the same kind of war, its debris is heaped in a different shape.

In the last days of our war its tragedy was to strike me with a sudden personal violence. My youngest brother, who had followed me into the Green Howards and had served on the Italian Front, was killed in France by a stray bullet. I knew his battalion had been transferred to the French Front, but I had had no particular anxiety for him: he was so young and vivid that the mind could not entertain his image and death's together. I was back in England at the time, stationed at Middlesbrough among strangers; but perhaps I was grateful for this isolation. My grief was too violent to tolerate sympathy or consolation. I walked about blinded by tears. I remember that I fled from the Garrison Headquarters and sought the seclusion of a park in the town. For the first and the only time I sought to expel my emotions by actualizing them in verse. It was a bleak October day, with the emblems of death and grief around me. The lines of an elegy came spontaneously to my mind:

> The autumn leaves were an augury
> And seemed to intend
> As they yellowly drooped in the languid air

THE IMPACT OF WAR

That life was a fragile mood and death
A tremendous despair.

The yellow leaves fell
Like slow tears of gold on the face of the day:
They fell to the earth with a faint, sad sigh.
They sighed /
As the feet of the passers-by
Crushed them into the moist, black soil.
They sighed when the gentle wind
Lifted them along the way.

In the Park
Old men swept the dead things in a heap to burn:
Their last fragrance
Floated about the naked trees.
I thought as the women walked in the moist, still day
Wearing yellow chrysanthemums in their coats,
A chrysanthemum was
A pale, disheveled emblem of death.

The sun
Was a silver pervasion across the sky:
From the sky
The dead leaves fell.

There was a good deal more of the poem, angry and
resentful, and vainly consolatory; but too raw for publication even at this distance of time. When the Armistice came,
a month later, I had no feelings, except possibly of self-
congratulation. By then I had been sent to dreary barracks
on the outskirts of Canterbury. There were misty fields

around us, and perhaps a pealing bell to celebrate our victory. But my heart was numb and my mind dismayed: I turned to the fields and walked away from all human contacts.

6

THE RAID

IT WAS early summer and the warm sun seemed to re-
animate the desolate land. Before one of a group of huts
a young subaltern was seated at a table. He was bareheaded
and the sun played on the bright yellow strands of his hair.
He played nervously with a match-stalk, splintering it with
his fingernails, scraping it aimlessly about the table. The
sun played on the white bleached wood of the twirling
match-stalk and on the dark blistered polish of the table.
Nervous fingers rolled the hard stalk between soft plastic
flesh. At times everything was very still. The dreamer
wandered. The shreds of match-stalk seemed far away,
brittle legs of birds, pattering on the hard brown table.
The sun was buoyed in some kind of space, hard to conceive; where, too, the mind swayed in utter helplessness.

Why had all the horror suddenly become potent? Lieutenant P—— had been in France four months now, and all
the time, in some degree, his life had been threatened. He
had been sick, sick all the time—but the hunted life had
each day sunk into renewing sleep; and day had succeeded
day, and somehow the faith had been born that the days
would pass in such a succession until the long terror was

ended. But the present eventuality had made a difference. He had been selected to lead a raid, along with me, and a volunteer party of about thirty men. This sudden actualization of the diffused terror of our existence had made a difference to my friend. I could divine it as he sat there in his restless abstraction.

I was lying within the hut, beneath the corrugated vault of iron. My body was listless, my mind content. I saw P——, crumpled in his chair—his boots drawn under, his untidy puttees, his rounded shoulders and over-big flaxen head. I saw men walking about the grassy plot in front of us, and in the sky, an easier reach for my recumbent eyes, a lark, a dot, a lark that was always singing in this region at the time of our stay there. The lark, and the men walking very near on a horizon, were more real to me than the vague wonder about my fate in the raid. I was afraid, but more interested in P——'s fear. I decided that he must in some way be imprisoned in his flesh—despite that mind, floating vacantly in the ether. He was an undersized but thickset man of about twenty-three. He had a pale fleshy face and china-blue eyes, a coarse voice and a tendency to blush. He had been a teacher. He had a mother and a sweetheart, and he spent a lot of time writing letters. He never got free from his home thoughts; he was still bound in some sort of personal dependence to these ties. His mind, at any rate, was not free to lead its own existence, or to create the conditions of its existence. I think that is why he was a coward.

For he was a coward, in the only concise sense that can be given to that word. A coward is not merely a man who feels fear. We all experience fear; it is a physical reaction to the

166

unknown extent of danger. But it is only cowardice when it becomes a mental reaction—when the mind, reacting to the flesh, submits to the instincts of the flesh.

As the time appointed for the raid grew nearer, P——'s manner began to change. We had always been thrown together a good deal: we were the only officers in the company with tastes in common. But we were scarcely friends; there was something physical in his nature which repelled me. But now he began to make up to me more insistently. Presently the remainder of the battalion went into the trenches and we were left to rest and train for our enterprise. P—— then grew more confidential and spoke often of his home affairs. He seemed afraid to be out of my presence. He began to confess to me; to bemoan his fate; to picture the odds against us—the utter unlikelihood that we should ever come out of this business alive.

I asked him if he was afraid. He blushed and said: 'Yes, damnably.' He was obviously in an agony of mind, and then I began to have my own fear: that he would bitch the show and bring disgrace on us all. I put this to him. We had left camp and were on a visit to battalion headquarters, a mile or two behind the line. There was some sort of gun emplacement or old trench line into which we had climbed to look out over the sunsoaked plain: the larks were singing as always in the still clear sky. But P——'s face looked aqueous and blotchy. His eyes were uneasy, reflecting all his anguish. After a while I asked him to make a clean breast of it all to the colonel. But I saw that he would never do that. He just hung his head and looked stupid.

When we reached the battalion I left P—— outside and

went into the colonel's shanty or dugout. I told about P——;
deliberately. He was immediately taken off the raid and
S——, an elderly subaltern who had already taken part in a
previous raid, was asked to take his place. This he did with
a bad grace.

P—— was killed in the end in a bombardment some
months later. A night of confused darkness and sudden riot.

We greased our hands and faces and then blackened them
with burned cork so that they would not shine out in the
dark night. We muffled our rifle slings and accoutrements so
that no little noise should betray us. Then we made our way
into the trenches to the point selected for our sally. A terrace
such as is often found in French fields ran across No Man's
Land, at right angles to the trenches. It led to an elbow in
the enemy's line, and the concerted plan was that at midnight exactly the artillery and trench mortars should isolate
this elbow with a barrage of fire, whilst we penetrated into
the trenches and secured some of the enemy, dead or alive.
We raiders were to creep along the guiding line of the
bank in Indian file until within thirty yards or so of the
enemy's position, then to creep round into a compact line
facing the trench: this movement to be achieved by midnight. Then, immediately the barrage fell, we were to rush
forward and do our best.

It was agreed that I should head the Indian file, and that
S—— should bring up the rear. He was to prevent straggling
and to see that the line swung round into position when I
sent back the signal. The last thing we did before going out
was to give each man a stiff dose of rum: then there were a

few whispered farewells and a handshake or two. The night was moonless, but fair, and not quite pitch dark. You could distinguish a silhouette against the skyline. As soon as we passed our own wire entanglements we got down on our bellies and began to crawl. I had already explored the ground in two or three special night patrols, and had no difficulty in finding the bank and getting the right direction. I advanced a step at a time, the sergeant close behind me.

I felt that I ought not to neglect a single aspect of that slow advance to the enemy's lines, for in those few minutes I experienced a prolonged state of consciousness during which I hung over a pit of fear, weighted down by a long and vivid anticipation of its nature, and now brought to the last tension by this silent agony of deliberate approach. Fear is more powerful in silence and loneliness, for then the mind is more open to the electric uprush of the animal. There is safety in action and unanimity in all the noisy riot of strife—until even that safety is beaten down by the pitiless continuance of physical shock, and then there is only safety in the mind again, if it rise like a holy ghost out of the raw stumps of the body.

I remember for a time feeling my heart unrulily beating in my breast, and a tight constriction at the throat. That was perhaps only excitement, or tense expectation of activity. It was not the shuddering groveling impulse, the sudden jet of pus into the thrilling blood stream, that would sometimes, on the sudden near detonation of a shell, poison one's humanity. That, as I have said, is the only real kind of fear—the purely physical reaction. From that state a few men can recover because they have minds that can surmount a physical state: an imaginative sense of equilibrium. *Imaginative*—it was the men of imagination that were, if any, the men of courage. The men of mere brute strength, the footballers and school captains, found no way out of the inevitable physical reaction. Their bodies broke in fear because the wild energy of the instinct was impinging on a brittle red wall of physical being. That was the feel of it, that was the reality. And P——? P—— was in another state of being. Because he had imagination he could visualize and thus anticipate this physical nature of fear. He could immerse himself in the imaginative embodiment of that animalistic impulse, and because he had no faith he had to succumb to that imaginative condition. Faith was the deepest reality we tested as we crawled for a few minutes along that bank—a few minutes that actually seemed an age. Faith was of many kinds. But essentially it was simply a level condition of the mind. It might be Christian—sometimes was, I observed. But more often it was just fatalistic, and by fatalism I mean a resolve to live in peace of mind, in possession of mind, despite any physical environment. Such was the faith, or philosophy, that belonged to a great body of men, and was held in very different degrees of intellectuality and passion. In some—they were the majority—it was a reversion to a primitive state of belief. Every bullet has its billet. What's the use of worryin'? But in others it was a subtler state of consciousness. The war seemed to annihilate all sense of individuality. The mass of it was so immense that oneself as a separate unit could not rationally exist. But there is a sense in which the death of individuality means the birth of personality. This truth is the basis of all sacrifice and martyrdom. A saint may die for his faith, but only because that faith is an expression of his personality. And so in the presence of danger, and in the immediate expectation of death, one can forget the body and its fears and exist wholly as a mind.

We had gone perhaps three parts of our way, when we heard the sound of men working. Muffled coughs, thuds, indefinite clinks. I was nonplused. The explanation did not immediately occur to me. It hadn't time. I had a sudden sick fear that we must return, empty-handed shameful fools. I think this thought and image lasted the brief interval I had for reflection. For immediately the sergeant tugged my leg and crept close to my ear. He indicated somehow the right. I turned my head. Two figures loomed indistinctly in the dark. Approaching us. 'We must rush them,' I whispered. The sergeant said: 'Right; you give the tip.' The two figures blundered nearer. I could see them hesitate on the other side of the rim of a shell-hole. My heart had suddenly become calm. I was filled with a great exaltation. My body didn't exist, save as a wonderfully unconscious mechanism. I gave a great inhuman cry and dashed forward, barking with my Colt at the shadowy figures not ten yards away. One gave a wild bestial shriek and fell into the darkness. The other fired. We dueled, there in the dark. But I ran on, impelled by an unknown energy, the sergeant by my side. Just then the concerted moment arrived. A dark rainbow of shells hissed through the sky. The flash and detonation of heavy shells. The pale wavering rockets of the star-shells, they curved round us, fell among us. In that incessant theatrical light I saw my enemy dash into the shell-hole at his feet and fall down crying for mercy. I had my foot on the squirming body, sergeant his bayonet. It was an officer. I perceived that quickly, clearly. It was enough. I gave the order: 'Back to the lines.' We turned. The barrage was over now. Only a blind hiss of bullets from the German line. We walked back to the trenches. My men came chattering round, peering with black faces at the prisoner. Prodding him with their bayonets. Crying happily. Lusting to kill him. I tried to keep them off. The prisoner was talking to me, wildly excited. At last he found his French. I understood. He was so pleased! Explained that he was married and had children. He wanted to live. I tried to calm him. He was a professor of philology and lived at Spandau. I took away his revolver; the sergeant took his bright dagger. And thus we reached our own line. As the German hesitated on the parapet someone kicked him violently on the backside, so that he fell down. I cursed the fellow, but didn't stop to identify him. S—— was there, waiting for me, very much mystified by the turn of events, but jubilant at the sight of a prisoner. We made our way to the headquarters' dugout and descended with our charge.

We blinked in the brilliant light of several candles. It was a square dugout with a fixed table served by benches from the walls. To get to the benches we had to crawl under the table. Our colonel was a Welshman, temporarily attached from another regiment. When away from the trenches he was pleasant enough, though at bottom a weak and emotional nature. We did not trust him, for he was known to be 'a white-livered funk.' A bottle of whisky was by him on the

table, as he sat facing the stairway. He had drunk a great
deal, for he was highly nervous about the result of the raid,
which would reflect on his reputation. He welcomed us
effusively. I don't remember all the chatter and confusion
in that confined space, but eventually some kind of order did
emerge. D——, our signaling officer, who knew German,
began to question the prisoner. The poor fellow was docile
enough. He gave up his letters, papers and maps, but asked
to keep a photograph of his wife, which we allowed. But a
more disgusting scene followed. He had on his finger a
signet-ring, perhaps rather a pretty one. The Colonel insisted
on having it, and because it would not pass the knuckle,
urged us to cut it off. The man was in a delirium and of
course we disregarded him. But he made efforts to reach
the prisoner himself and in the effort fell drunkenly over
and rolled under the table. He lay stupidly there and fell
asleep. I watched the prisoner. He was terribly excited, but
self-possessed. He was standing against the dark entrance,
speaking forcefully and at length. D—— explained to us at
intervals. He was passionately defending the German cause,
arguing persuasively that we, the English, had been faithless
to our common Teutonic stock. The future of Europe was
with the Germanic nations; they alone had the energy, the
fresh spirit, the nascent culture, for the creation of a new
world.

S—— left at about two o'clock to report particulars to the
Brigade Headquarters, and at dawn I set out with the prisoner and the happy raiders. We had lost only one man, and
there were no serious wounds. We filed down the communi-

cation trenches, leisurely enough, for we were tired. Our faces were still black with the charred cork. The sun rose up to greet us, and when finally we got out into the open country the day was warm and beneficent. The larks were singing again, as on my journey up with P——. But now the sky was pulsing with their shrill notes. On the way I talked to the prisoner, and once we rested for a while, sitting side by side on a fallen tree. He explained that when we first surprised them (he was a company officer with his orderly, visiting parties out at work on the battered wire entanglements) they had taken us for Senegalese troops, and his orderly's terror was perhaps largely due to this mistake. But we talked mostly of other things. I was eager to learn anything about their side—their state of mind, their public opinion, the possibility of revolution and an end of all this meaningless strife. Nietzsche was at that time still fresh in my awakening mind, and I stammered in broken enthusiasm about his books, but got no response. He was now too aware of his liberty, his safety, his bodily emancipation to think of such things. He was happy to be safe at last, but perhaps he was also a little chagrined. He was amazed at my youth and perhaps a little ashamed of being captured by what looked like a boyish prank. We strolled on again. I only recall his features with difficulty. He was fair and rather short. But I should not know him if I met him again.

When we reached the Brigade Headquarters I handed him over and stayed to watch him questioned. He stood at attention before a table in the open. And when this was done, he was given into the charge of a guard to be taken down to the Divisional Camp. I last saw him standing at a distance from me, waiting to move. I gazed at him eagerly, tenderly, for I had conceived some sort of vicarious affection for this man. I had done my best to kill him a few hours before. I waved my hand as he left, but he only answered with a vague smile.

I then made for my battalion reserve and found a hut and a bed. I slept for more than twelve hours and in my sleep, perhaps from weariness, or because of some relaxation in my nerves, my heart seemed to stop and my blood to sweep round in a dark red whirlpool. In my dream I wondered if this was death. But when I awoke I was fresh and content. I was alive. There was light streaming in through the windows, and friendly voices.

7

IN RETREAT

A JOURNAL OF THE RETREAT OF THE FIFTH ARMY FROM ST. QUENTIN, MARCH, 1918

I

WE RECEIVED the warning order just before dinner, and for a while talked excitedly round the mess fire, some scoffing at the idea of an imminent battle, others gravely saying that this time at any rate the warning was justified. Two deserters, with tales of massing guns and the night-movements of innumerable troops, had reached our lines the previous day. Of course, deserters usually had some such tale designed to tempt a captor's leniency, but this time it was likely to be the truth. What else could the enemy's long silence mean? To that question we had no answer. We went early to bed, expecting an early awakening. The harnessed horses stood in lowered shafts.

There was scarcely a wall standing in Fluquières: everywhere demolition and bombardment had reduced the village to irregular cairns of brick and plaster. Winding among these cairns were the cleared roadways. Men and horses rested in patched sheds and an occasional cellar. S—— and I were in a small repaired stable, each with a bed-frame in a manger. I had livened the cleanly white-washed walls of the place with illustrations from a colored magazine. That evening all save our trench-kit had been sent to the transport-wagons, and we were lying on the bare netting with only our trench coats thrown over us.

For some time I was too excited to sleep, and none too warm. But weariness did at length triumph, and when, a short while afterwards, I was roughly awakened, I had become unconscious enough to forget the continuity of things.

II

Yes: suddenly I was awake. A match was being applied to the candle stuck on the bed-frame above my head. With his excited face illumined in the near candle-light, an orderly bent over me and shook my shoulders. I heard confused shoutings, and the rumble of gunfire. I had hardly need to read the message-form held out to me: 'Man Battle Stations' —the code words I knew only too well, and all that they implied. I was shivering violently with the cold, but in the shaking candle-light I scribbled messages repeating the code to the company commanders, the transport officer, and to others. S—— was moving on the other side of the wall that divided the mangers.

'We're in for it, my lad,' he yelled, above the increasing din.

Just then there was the sudden shrieking rush of a descending shell and its riotous detonation very near. Our candles jumped out, and we were in darkness, with bricks and earth falling like a hail on the roof. My servant came in, and hastily helped me to gather my equipment together. He handled the two or three books I always carried with me, asking me if I would take one in my pocket. I took Thoreau's *Walden,* because I had not yet read it, and anticipated two or three weary days of passive defense. For even if now we realized the actuality of the enemy's attack, so confident were we of our defensive system that we contemplated nothing more than a short successful resistance. When in the front line, we had ceaselessly reconnoitered all approaches, and so fine were the sweeping fields of fire that stretched away towards St. Quentin, so skillfully placed were our machine-guns, that always we pitied the folly of the enemy should he assail a defense so deadly. We reckoned with one factor unseen.

I fixed my revolver and ammunition securely, and set out to the orderly room, some five hundred yards away. It was now about five o'clock and still dark. I picked my way along a path which led across the great heaps of rubble. Shells were falling in the village. I still shivered with cold. My electric torch was nearly exhausted, so that I kept falling as I went. When I reached the orderly room, which was in a restored cottage, I found everything in a great hubbub, orderlies coming and going, the sergeant-major shouting orders. Inside, the doctor was bandaging a wounded man.

S——, who had been assembling the headquarter staff, came to say that something terrible had happened to the Lewis team (at that time a Lewis-gun team was attached to each battalion headquarters): would I come round with my torch.

178

They had been sleeping, some six men, beneath tarpaulin sheets, stretched across a half-demolished out-house. A shell had fallen in the middle of them. In the weak glare of my torch, we saw a mangled mass of red brick-dust and of red glistening blood. Here and there we distinguished a tousled head of hair. One man, pinned beneath beams and brick-work, was still groaning. We quickly began to extricate him, but he died while we worked.

I then joined the colonel, and with one or two orderlies and the sergeant-major we followed the companies along the back lane that led from Fluquières to Roupy, a distance of about a mile and a half. The morning was cold and a heavy dew lay on the ground. As we walked the light of dawn began to reveal a thick wet mist.

III

At 6.50 I sent a message to the brigade, informing them that the battalion was in position. We had been shelled all along the way, and when we neared Roupy, the cross-roads seemed to be under a continuous barrage. Nevertheless, we got into position with very few casualties. Safe in the bowels of the headquarter dugout, we thought the worst was over, and began casually to eat the tongue-sandwiches and drink the tea provided by the mess-corporal.

The dugout was new and spacious, and odorous of the fresh chalky earth. It was about thirty feet deep, and partitioned into three sections, of which the middle one was occupied by the headquarter officers. Because it was new it was unfurnished, and we had to squat on the bare floor, grouped round a few candles.

For me that cavern is a telephonic nightmare. The instrument, a 'D III converted,' was placed on the floor in a corner of the dugout. Two signalers sat with their legs straddling round it. At first the companies, then the neighboring battalions, and, finally, the brigade, kept me there crouching on the floor, yelling till I was hoarse into the execrable instrument. When I was not speaking, the signalers were receiving or sending Morse messages.

Above the ground the situation was disquieting. The thick mist of the early dawn persisted: a man ten yards away could not be distinguished. The gunfire, tremendous in its intensity, continued hour after hour to pound into the invisible foreground. The earth vibrated almost hysterically. An occasional shell crashed near us, but after the first three hours (at 7.30) the enemy's fire seemed to be concentrated on our front-line defenses. No messages, telephonic or written, came to relieve our anxiety.

The gradual accumulation of our anxiety should be realized. Every minute seemed to add to its intensity. By ten o'clock or so, our hearts were like taut drum skins beaten reverberantly by every little incident.

Then the skin smashed. Bodily action flickered like flame, the sense of duration was consumed away.

Shortly after eleven o'clock, a gun team galloped madly down the main road. Then two stragglers belonging to the Machine-Gun Corps were brought to headquarters. They informed us that the front line had been penetrated. Later, an officer from the front line battalion, with five or six men, came to us out of the mist. Most of the party were wounded, and as the officer's leg was being bandaged in the dugout, he told us his tale. He was haggard and incoherent, but the sequence was awfully clear to us. The enemy had attacked in great strength at 7.30. They had apparently reached the observation line unobserved, and overpowered the few men there before a warning could be given or an escape made. Advancing under cover of a creeping barrage, they had approached the main line of defense. No fire met them there, or only fire directed vaguely into the fog. The fight at the main line had been short and bloody. Our men, dazed and quivering after three hours' hellish bombardment (I could see them cowering on the cold mist-wet earth), had been brave to the limits of heroism; but pitifully powerless. The ghastly job had been completed by 8.30. About nine o'clock fresh enemy battalions passed through their fellows and advanced towards the front-line redoubt (L'Épine de Dallon). Our artillery fire must have been useless by then, still falling on the old enemy front line. At any rate, the enemy quickly surrounded the redoubt, and then penetrated it. This officer himself had been captured, and later had made his escape in the mist. He thought it possible that the headquarters of his battalion were still holding out.

We were still questioning our informant when an excited voice yelled down the dugout shaft: 'Boches on the top of the dugout.' Our hearts thumped. There was no reason why the enemy shouldn't be on us. They might have been anywhere in that damned mist. We drew our revolvers and rushed to the shaft. We did not mean to be caught like rats in a hole.

I remember my emotion distinctly: a quiet despair. I *knew* I went up those stairs either to be shot or bayoneted as I emerged, or, perhaps, to be made prisoner and so plunge into a strange unknown existence.

Half-way up the stairs, and a voice cried down: 'It's all right: they're our fellows.' Some artillerymen in overcoats, straggling across the open, had looked sinister in the mist.

We turned to the dugout, the released tension leaving us exhausted.

Patrols from our front companies had been feeling outward all morning, at first without result. At 12.30 B—— (commanding the left front company) reported: 'Machine-gun and rifle-fire on left and right can be heard. Shelling very hard. Can see nothing. Patrols are being sent out.' At 1 P.M. he reported: 'Boche are in quarry just in front of me. We are firing Lewis guns and rifles at him. He seems to be firing from our right flank too, with machine-guns.'

These and other messages all came by runner. The telephonic communications to the companies had broken down before noon, though I think we remained in touch with the brigade until late in the afternoon.

About midday the mist began to clear a little. At one o'clock the enemy, having massed in the valley five hundred yards immediately in front of us, attacked in mass strength. The fusillade that met them must have been terrific. They came on in good order, extending and maneuvering with precision. At 1.20 B—— reported: 'No. 5 Platoon report enemy on wire in front. Artillery assistance is asked for. We are firing rifle grenades into them.' And again at 1.30 'Boche attacking in strength with sections in front. Front troops are in valley in front. They are also heading to my left flank.' Between 1.30 and 1.40 the attack reached its greatest intensity. By 1.45 it had withered completely before the hail of our fire.

At 1.45 B—— reported: 'Boche running back like hell near Savy. They seem to be running from artillery as much as anything.' (Savy was one and a half miles to our left front: it was on the slope that rose away from the valley in front of us where the enemy had massed his forces before his attack.)

For a moment we became elated. There was cause enough. The mist had lifted, and a pale sun shone. We had defeated a strong attack. We received a message from the Inniskillings on our right to say they still held their positions intact. And wider afield the co-ordination of the enemy's advance seemed to have broken down.

We made haste to distribute our reserve ammunition, to clear the dressing-station, and generally to make ourselves ready for the next happenings.

In reply to my inquiries B—— sent this message, timed 2.15 P.M.: 'It is very difficult to tell numbers of enemy. I can see the ground north to Savy, and saw them scattered. The line advancing had about 30 men to every 100 yards. We do not require S.A.A. yet. Can you instruct Rose * to fire up Soup Valley, please? We will want Verey lights for the night. Will a supply be forthcoming? Can see no movement now. Boche is putting up white lights all along valley.'

IV

The lull was not of long duration. Either we had been deceived by the movements near Savy, or the enemy had made a miraculously swift recovery. At 2.45 I received an-

* Code name for a company.

other message from B——: 'Enemy movement at F—— 12 at 4.0. They appear to be carrying in wounded. Enemy also advancing across valley on left on F—— 5, in small parties. Estimated total strength seen, 50 men. Boche airplanes are flying about 300 feet above our lines, and have been for a short while past. There is still some machine-gun fire in front. Is a redoubt holding out?'

The airplanes were evidently making a preliminary re-connaissance, and I guessed the movement to be significant of a new attack.

On the mists clearing, the airplanes were able to sight position, and soon the artillery on both sides became active. Our own artillery, alas, fired short, smashing our already weakened defenses. The Germans brought up their light field guns with great skill and rapidity. Several batteries were observed coming over the ridge at L'Épine de Dallon —only a few hours ago the headquarters of the battalion we were supporting. We now realized our position in earnest, and I sent a detailed account of the situation to the brigade.

Towards four o'clock, the enemy shelling increased in intensity. The second attack was now imminent. B—— sent the following message, timed 4.30 P.M. 'Boche is attacking on right about 400 strong, and is massing in the valley right in front of Roupy. We want some more S.A.A. During the Boche retreat the riflemen and Lewis guns did good work, killing many. Shelling very heavy.'

The heavy shelling continued, and under cover of its intensity the enemy again massed in the valley in front of us. The men held on grimly. Thus B——, timed 5.10 P.M.: 'Line holding still with some casualties. Reports not in.

Line heavily shelled. S.A.A. received correct. Situation still the same. Touch is being kept with battalion on our right, and patrols go constantly. Our chloride of lime is missing and cannot be found. Machine-guns very active.' And again at 5.40 P.M.: 'The Boche is 50 yards or less from our line, and is also passing down the valley for another attack.'

Then suddenly those massed men leaped from cover, and came on in their gray, regular formations. At headquarters we were only aware of the angry surge of rifle and machine-gun fire, deadening even the detonations of shells. All this time I was spending tiring, exasperating hours at the telephone, striving to get in communication with brigade and artillery headquarters. Again and again the wire was broken, and again and again the linesmen went out into the mist to mend it. Then it got disconnected irreparably. We were isolated in that chaos.

About 6.30 B—— sent the following momentous message: 'Boche got inside our wire on right and left. No. 5 Platoon are all either wiped out or prisoners. No. 7 Platoon took up position on left of keep, but Boche were in it when I left. They also were in trench on right of road left by C Company, and we killed several on road near camouflage. I am now in redoubt with 25 men.'

The climax had come. We had still one card to play—the counter-attack company. On receipt of B——'s message, the colonel decided to order C—— to attack in accordance with the pre-conceived plan.

We only heard of this counter-attack from the mouths of a few survivors. It was one of the most heroic episodes in the retreat. The company gathered together in the shell-battered trench that they had occupied all day, and then took the open. No artillery covered their advance. It was hopeless, insane, suicidal. They had perhaps one hundred and fifty yards to cover. They advanced at a jog-trot, lumbering on the uneven ground. One by one they fell before the fusillade that met them. C—— had reached the enemy with about a dozen men. These leaped in among the Boches, and a hand-to-hand struggle ensued for a few minutes. C—— was last seen cursing, pinned to the trench wall by a little mob of Germans, in one hand his empty smoking revolver.

V

It was now dusk, and with dusk came peace and silence. And at dusk this was our position:—The front rim of the redoubt was in the enemy's possession. The counter-attack company had disappeared. The company-keeps still held out with a few men in each. The inner ring of the redoubt was held by one company, and the remnants of three. B—— had survived with one of his officers. But several officers in the three front companies had been either killed, wounded, or captured. There were probably two hundred men still sur-viving in the battalion.

In the darkness the colonel and I walked up to the line. As we went along the road, the stillness was abruptly broken by the sound of three or four shots, screams and curses. We flung ourselves on the roadside, our revolvers ready. We shouted: 'Who goes there?' English voices answered, and the sergeant-major went to investigate. Two German privates had walked into a sentry on the road, *coming from behind us.* No one could understand what they said, and they were sent back to brigade headquarters. And I don't remember that any one of us was perturbed by the incident, eerie though it was.

Just after one o'clock in the day, we received long-awaited instructions from the brigade. The battalion in reserve was to deliver a counter-attack. The line of deployment was given, and the direction of attack. The battalion was to leave its position at 12.45, and the guns were to start a creeping barrage at 1.33 A.M.

The whole thing was a ghastly failure. The night was black, and the battalion attacking was unfamiliar with the ground it had to cover. We waited hours for a sign of their approach. About two o'clock a stray officer came to us, having lost his company. Eventually, about four o'clock, one company did appear. It went forward in the darkness, but got dispersed and uncontrollable in the effort to deploy into attack formation. Dawn found us as dusk had found us, with the sole difference that some two hundred men of the counter-attack battalion had found refuge in our redoubt, and in the keeps in front.

I think by then we were past hope or despair. We regarded all events with an indifference of weariness, knowing that with the dawn would come another attack. We distributed ammunition, reorganized our Lewis guns, and waited dully, without apprehension.

Again the morning was thickly misty. Our own artillery fire was desultory and useless. Under cover of the mist, the enemy massed in battle formation, and the third attack began about 7 A.M. We only heard a babel in the mist. Now our artillery was firing short among our men in the redoubt.

About ten o'clock the enemy penetrated our left flank, presumably in the gap between us and the battalion on our left, which was still in position. Machine-gun fire began to harass us from that direction, somewhere in the ruins of the village. We never heard from the battalion on our right, and a runner I sent there did not return. I think they must have withdrawn about ten o'clock.

This new attack petered out. I fancy it was only half-hearted on the part of the enemy—probably only a demonstration to see if we intended to make a determined resistance, or to fight only a rearguard action. Finding the resistance determined enough, they evidently retired to prepare the real thing.

This fourth attack was delivered about midday. The mist still persisted thinly. One could perhaps see objects fifty yards away. I don't know what resistance the platoon-keeps offered. They were in a hopeless position, and would easily have been swamped in a massed attack.

Shortly after midday, the enemy came in direct contact with the inner ring of the redoubt.

We fired like maniacs. Every round of ammunition had been distributed. The Lewis guns jammed; rifle bolts grew stiff and unworkable with the expansion of heat.

In the lull before noon, the colonel and I had left the dugout, in which we were beginning to feel like rats in a trap, and had found an old gun-pit about two hundred and fifty yards farther back, and here we established our headquarters. An extraordinary thing happened. The gun-pit was dug out of the bank on the roadside. About two o'clock one of our guns, evidently assuming that Roupy had been evacuated, began to pound the road between Roupy and Fluquières. One of these shells landed clean on the road edge of our pit. We were all hurled to the ground by the explosion, but, on recovering ourselves, found only one casualty: the colonel had received a nasty gash in the forearm. We then went two hundred to three hundred yards across the open, away from the road, and found a smaller overgrown pit. The colonel refused to regard his wound as serious; but he soon began to feel dizzy, and was compelled to go back to the dressing-station. I was then left in charge of the battalion.

It was now about 2.30. The attack still persisted in a guerilla fashion. But the enemy was massing troops in the trenches already taken. At 4 p.m. the intensity of the attack deepened suddenly. A new intention had come into the enemy's mind: he was directing his attack on the flanks of our position in an effort to close round us like pincers. On the left he made use of cover offered by the ruined village, and eventually brought machine-guns to bear against us from our left rear. On the right he made use of the trenches evacuated by the Inniskillings.

In the height of this attack, while my heart was heavy with anxiety, I received a message from the brigade. Surely reinforcements were coming to our aid! Or was I at length given permission to withdraw? Neither: it was a rhetorical appeal to hold on to the last man. I rather bitterly resolved to obey the command.

Another hour passed. The enemy pressed on relentlessly with a determined, insidious energy, reckless of cost. Our position was now appallingly precarious. I therefore resolved to act independently, and do as perhaps I should have done hours earlier. I ordered B—— to organize a withdrawal. This message dispatched, I lay on my belly in the grass and watched through my field-glasses every minute trickling of the enemy's progress. Gradually they made their way round the rim of the redoubt, bombing along the traverses. And now we only held it as lips might touch the rim of a saucer. I could see the heads of my men, very dense and in a little space. And on either side, incredibly active, gathered the gray helmets of the Germans. It was like a long bowstring along the horizon, and our diminished forces the arrow to be shot into a void. A great many hostile machine-guns had now been brought up, and the plain was sprayed with hissing bullets. They impinged and spluttered about the little pit in which I crouched.

I waited anxiously for B—— to take the open. I saw men crawl out of the trenches, and lie flat on the parados, still firing at the enemy. Then, after a little while, the arrow was launched. I saw a piteous band of men rise from the ground, and run rapidly towards me. A great shout went up from the Germans: a cry of mingled triumph and horror. 'Halt Eenglisch!' they cried, and for a moment were too amazed to fire; as though aghast at the folly of men who could plunge into such a storm of death. But the first silent gasp of horror expended, then broke the crackling storm. I don't remember in the whole war an intenser taste of hell. My men came along spreading rapidly to a line of some two hundred yards length, but bunched here and there. On the left, by the main road, the enemy rushed out to cut them off. Bayonets clashed there. Along the line men were falling swiftly as the bullets hit them. Each second they fell, now one crumpling up, now two or three at once. I saw men stop to pick up their wounded mates, and as they carried them along, themselves get hit and fall with their inert burdens. Now they were near me, so I rushed out of my pit and ran with them to the line of trenches some three hundred yards behind.

It seemed to take a long time to race across those few hundred yards. My heart beat nervously, and I felt infinitely weary. The bullets hissed about me, and I thought: then this is the moment of death. But I had no emotions. I remembered having read how in battle men are hit, and never feel the hurt till later, and I wondered if I had yet been hit. Then I reached the line. I stood petrified, enormously aghast. *The trench had not been dug, and no reinforcements occupied it.* It was as we had had passed it on the morning of the 21st, the sods dug off the surface, leaving an immaculately patterned 'mock' trench. A hundred yards on the right a machine-gun corps had taken up a position, and was already covering our retreat. I looked about me wildly, running along the line and signaling to the men to drop as they reached the slender parapet of sods. But the whole basis of my previous tactics had been destroyed. I should never have ordered my men to cross that plain of death, but for the expectation that we were falling back to reinforce a new line. We found an empty mockery, and I was in despair. But I must steady the line. On the actual plain the men obeyed my signals, and crouched in the shallow trench. But even as they crouched, the bullets struck them. On the road, the straight white road leading to the western safety, there was something like a stampede. S—— and the sergeant-major went and held it with pointed revolvers. But it was all useless—hopeless. On the right, I saw the enemy creeping round. They would soon enfilade us, and then our shallow defense would be a death-trap. I accordingly gave the signal to withdraw, bidding the two Lewis guns to cover us as long as possible. Once more we rose and scattered in retreat. It would be about seven hundred yards to the next trenches— the village line round Fluquières—and this we covered fairly well, sections occasionally halting to give covering fire. The enemy had not yet ventured from the redoubt, and our distance apart was now great enough to make his fire of little effect. And I think as we moved up the slope towards the village we must have been in 'dead' ground, so far as the enemy advancing on the right was concerned.

We reached Fluquières, which lay on the top of the slope, and found there some deep trenches on each side of the road at the entrance of the village. Further to the left, I found certain London troops commanded by a major. One of my Lewis guns still remained intact, and this I placed to fire down the straight road to Roupy. The enemy had now left the redoubt and were advancing in line formation.

We were at Fluquières about an hour. The enemy evidently did not intend to rest content with his capture of the redoubt. It was just beginning to get dusk. Earlier we had noticed sporadic contact lights go up. But now they shot into the sky from all along the plain. Low-flying airplanes hovered over the advancing line, and their wireless messages soon put the German guns on to us. Big black high-explosive shells began to fall on our position, making our tired flesh shudder. I now began to be amazed at the advancing contact lights. They did not merely stretch in a line in front of us: *they encircled us like a horse-shoe, the points of which seemed* (and actually were) *miles behind us*. On the right the enemy was enfilading us with machine-gun fire.

I searched for the major commanding the troops on my left, but could not find him. By this time I was determined to act, and therefore gave the order to withdraw. The men filed through the village, gathering fresh ammunition from a dump at the cross-roads. From the village the road went up a slope leading to Aubigny. The enemy's fire soon followed us, and we proceeded along the ditches on each side of the road.

Three-quarters of the way up the slope I observed a trench running at right angles to the road on each side of it. I ordered the London men to go to the left, my own to the right, there to reorganize into companies. The twilight was now fairly deep, and I thought that with evening the enemy's advance would stay. The major I had seen in Fluquières now appeared again, and cursed me for giving the order to retire. I was too tired to argue, and even then a gust of machine-gun fire swept above our heads. They were going to attack again. We could hear them moving in the semi-darkness. Something else we could hear too—the throb of a motor cycle behind us. It was a dispatch rider, and when he drew level to us, he stopped his machine and came towards me with a message. I opened it. It ordered all troops east of the Aubigny defenses to retire through Ham.

I was glad. I believe I thought then that it was the end of our share in the battle. I went to the men, and assembled them in companies, and in close artillery formation we retired across country due west. We came to the Aubigny defenses, manned by fresh troops, about a mile further on, and then we gathered on the road again and marched wearily along. I remember coming to a water-tank, where we all drank our fill—our mouths were swollen with thirst. When we reached Ham, an officer met us and ordered us to proceed to Muille Villette, about two miles further on, and there billet for the night. Ham, as we walked through its cobbled streets, seemed very hollow and deserted. The last time we had seen it, it had been a busy market-town, full of civilians. Now only a few sinister looters went about the empty houses with candles. We saw one fellow come out of a door with a lady's reticule and other things over his arm. We should have been justified in shooting him, but we were far too tired. We just noticed him stupidly.

The road seemed long, and our pace was slow, but at last we reached the village of Muille Villette. We found it full of artillery men, and a few infantry. Every available shelter seemed to be occupied, but at length we got the men into a school. Our transport had been warned of our station for the night, and turned up with bully-beef and biscuits. These we served out.

I had four officers left with me. We could not find a billet for ourselves, but finally begged for shelter in a barn occupied by artillery men. They looked on us unsympathetically, not knowing our experiences. On a stove one of them was cooking a stew of potatoes and meat, and its savor made us lusting beasts. But the artillery men ate the slop unconcernedly, while we lay down too utterly weary to sleep, languidly chewing bully-beef.

VI

It was after midnight when we came to Muille Villette; I suppose about 2 A.M. we fell into an uneasy sleep. At 4 A.M. we were awakened by the stirrings and shoutings of the artillerymen. I drew my long boots on my aching feet, and went out into the cold darkness. I found an officer of some kind. The enemy were reported to have attacked and penetrated the Aubigny defenses, and to be now advancing on Ham. All the troops stationed in Muille Villette had received orders to withdraw.

We assembled the men, stupid with sleep. I knew that brigade headquarters were stationed at Golancourt, a mile and a half along the road. I resolved to proceed there and ask for orders. We marched away while the dawn was breaking.

I found the brigade established in a deserted house. T——, the brigade-major, was seated on a bed lacing his boots. No orders for the brigade had yet been received, so T—— advised me to find billets for the men, where they could rest and get food. The companies then sought billets independently, and, what was more blessed than anything, we managed to get them hot tea. I went and had breakfast with the brigade staff. The tea revived me, and I remember how voracious I felt, and that I tried to hide this fact. The brigadier came into the room and seemed very pleased to see me: apparently he was very satisfied with our conduct, and especially with the frequent reports I had sent back. Till then I had only felt weariness and bafflement—even shame. But now I began to see that we were implicated in something immense—something beyond personal feelings and efforts.

The brigadier told me as much as he knew of the general situation. It was not much. The communications had apparently broken down. But it was enough to make me realize that more than a local attack was in progress: the whole of the Fifth Army was involved: but there were no limits to what *might* be happening.

I also learned that Drury—where the divisional headquarters had been stationed—a village some five or six miles south-*west* of Roupy, had been captured about two o'clock on the afternoon of the 22nd, several hours before we had evacuated the redoubt. Only a miracle of chance had saved us from being cut off.

The brigade seemed to have difficulty in getting into touch with the division, or, at any rate, in obtaining orders from them. But at 10 A.M. I was told to march to Freniches and await orders there. We assembled in the village street and marched on again. The road was busy with retreating artillery and a few infantrymen. From behind us came the sounds of firing: the enemy were attacking Ham. We trudged on, passing villages whose inhabitants were only just taking steps to flee. They piled beds, chairs, and innumerable bolsters on little carts, some hand-pulled, some yoked to bony horses. They tied cows behind. There were old men, many old women, a few young women, but no young men. They and their like proceeded with us along the western road.

We had gone perhaps five miles when an orderly on horseback overtook us with orders. We were to report to the ——th Division at Freniches.

This we eventually did, and a fat staff colonel studied a

map, and then told me to take my battalion to Esmery-Hallon, a village four miles due north, and there take up a defensive position. This was more than I expected. I explained that my men had been fighting continuously for forty-eight hours, and were beaten and spiritless. But I received no comfort: the situation demanded that every available man should be used to the bitter end. I hardly dared to face my men: but I think they were too tired to mind where they went. We turned off at a right angle, and slowly marched on. The road led through a beautiful patch of country, steeped in a calm, liquid sunshine. We tilted our bodies forward, and forced our weary muscles to act.

About two miles south of Esmery-Hallon, an officer (a lieutenant) appeared on a motor cycle. He was in command of a scrap lot—transport men, cobblers, returned leave men, etc. He seemed to have the impression that the enemy were upon us, and wanted me to deploy and take up a position facing east. I explained that we were much too tired to do any such thing. He expostulated. Did I realize this, that, and the other? I explained that I had cause to realize such things better than he did. He raved. I told him finally that I didn't care a damn, but that I had orders to defend Esmery-Hallon, and hither I must go. He went off in a rage, seeming incredibly silly and fussy to us all.

Esmery-Hallon is a small village perched on a detached conical hill, overlooking the plain on all sides. The defense was simply arranged. Two companies of engineers were entrenched in front of the village. I sent a lookout on to the top of the church tower, and extended my men astraddle the hill on each side of the village, north and south. The men on the south found a ditch, which made an admirable trench. The men on the north extended over the plowed land, and dug shallow pits for shelter. We had no machine-guns or Lewis guns, but every man had a rifle and a decent amount of ammunition. I established my headquarters on the north side by a quarry, where I had a wide view of the plain.

The day was very still, and the distant rattle of machine-gun fire carried to us. A few enemy shells fell ineffectively about the landscape. I got into touch with a major of the Inniskillings in command of one hundred and fifty men on my right, and we co-ordinated defenses on that wing. My left wing was in the air, so to speak—not a soul visible for miles.

When our dispositions were finally made, I returned to the quarry edge. My batman T—— had already been away to search the village, and now came laden with samples of red wine and cider which he had found in a cellar. So I sent him back to the village with other men, telling them to search for food also. They soon returned with bottles of red wine and a large tin of army biscuits. Evidently there was any amount of wine, but I was afraid to distribute it among the men for fear lest on fasting stomachs it should make them drunk. So S—— and I each took a wine glass, and starting at different points, we began to go a round of the men. Each man lay curled up in his shallow pit, resting. To each we gave a glass of wine and a few biscuits. They took it thankfully. There was a lull in the distant fighting: I don't remember any noise of fire during that hour. The sun was warm and seemed to cast a golden peace on the scene. A feeling of unity with the men about me suddenly suffused my mind.

VII

It was nearly two o'clock when we got settled. About this time I interrupted a message which gave me the useful information that the enemy had been seen in Ham at 10 A.M. I guessed that the silence meant they were now consolidating along the Somme Canal. Later in the afternoon a cavalry patrol trotted up to our position. Officer, men, and horses all looked very debonair and well fed. The officer was very condescending towards me, but made a message of the information I gave him, thought it would not be worth while venturing further on to the plain, so rode away back, harness jingling, the sun shining on well-polished accoutrements.

About five o'clock, I judged that we were to be left alone for the night, and made my plans accordingly. I sent the following message to B——, who was in charge of the men on the right of the village: 'We hold on to our present positions unless otherwise ordered. When it is getting dark close your men in a little to form about 7 or 8 pickets. From these pickets send standing patrols out about 150 yards, or to any good observation point within warning distance. Any show of resistance should drive off any enemy patrols. But as far as I can make out the Boche is still east of the canal. Should you be attacked by overwhelming numbers, withdraw fighting in a due westerly direction under your own arrangements. I should do the same in case of need. I suggest you come up to have a look at our position before dark.'

But just after dark, I received orders to relieve the Royal Engineers in front of the village. I regretted this order, but had to obey it. We now found ourselves in freshly dug trenches on the flat of the plain, our view to the left and right obstructed by woods.

Included in the orders mentioned was a message to the effect that advance parties of the French would probably arrive that night, and the positions would be shown to them. This message filled us with wild hope; we became almost jaunty.

But the night was very cold, and heavily wet with dew. We improved the trenches, and stamped about, flapping our arms in an effort to keep warm. I sat with L——, bravest and brightest of my runners, on a waterproof sheet beneath a tree in the center of our position. We waited for the dawn: it was weird, phantasmagorical. Again the fateful mist. As it cleared a little, the woods near us hung faintly in the whiteness.

At 8 A.M. we began to observe troops retreating in front of us. They came in little groups down the road, or straggled singly over the landscape. The mist gradually lifted. We heard machine-gun fire fairly near, somewhere on the right. The stragglers informed us that the enemy had crossed the canal in the early dawn, and was advancing in considerable force. We waited patiently. At 9 A.M. the enemy came into touch with our fellows on the left, and here we rebutted him successfully. At 9.30 the troops on our right were reported to be withdrawing. About ten o'clock, there happened one of those sudden episodes, which would be almost comic with their ludicrous *bouleversement* were they not so tragic in their results. Seemingly straight from the misty sky itself, but in reality from our own guns, descended round after round of shrapnel bursting terrifically just above our heads, and spraying leaden showers upon us. Simultaneously, from the woods on our right, there burst a fierce volley of machine-gun fire, hissing and spluttering among us. We just turned and fled into the shelter of the village buildings. I shouted to my men to make for the position of the quarry. We scuttled through gardens and over walls. By the time we reached the quarry we had recovered our nerve. We extended and faced the enemy, who were advancing skillfully over the plain on our left. We on our part were a scrap lot composed of various units. We hastily reorganized into sections. Retreat was inevitable. Then followed a magnificent effort of discipline. A major took charge of the situation, and we began to retire with covering fire, section by section, in perfect alternation.

We were now on a wide expanse of plain, sloping gently westward. We stretched over this—a thin line of men, perhaps a thousand yards long. We were approaching the Nesle-Noyon Canal. When within a few hundred yards of the canal, we closed inwards to cross a bridge (Ramecourt). At the other end of the bridge stood a staff officer, separating the men like sheep as they crossed, first a few to the left, then a few to the right. Here I got separated from the majority of my men, finding myself with only fifteen. We were told to proceed along the bank of the canal until we found an unoccupied space, and there dig in.

As we crossed the bridge, we saw for the first time the sky-blue helmets of French troops peeping above a parapet. I think our eyes glistened with expectation of relief.

We went perhaps half a mile along the bank of the canal, and there I halted my attenuated company. The sun was now blazing hotly above our heads. We dropped to the ground, utterly exhausted. Presently some of the men began spontaneously to dig. R——, the only officer left with me, also took a pick and joined the men. I began to feel ashamed just then, for I would willingly have died. I took a spade (there was a dump of such things just by us) and began to shovel the earth loosened by R——. I seemed to be lifting utterly impossible burdens. My flesh seemed to move uneasily through iron bands; my leaden lids drooped smartingly upon my eyes.

We dug about three feet, and then ceased, incapable of more. At the foot of the bank there was a small pool of water. The enemy was not now in sight, so we plunged our hot faces and hands into its weedy freshness, and took off our boots and socks, and bathed our aching feet.

In the evening, about 5 P.M., a few skirmishing patrols appeared on the horizon. But our artillery was now active and fairly accurate, and machine-guns swept the plain. The patrols retired, without having advanced any distance. A large German airplane, with a red belly, floated persistently above our line. We fired hundreds of shots at it, but without effect. T——, my batman, nearly blew my head off in his efforts.

We had gathered a lot of sun-scorched hemlock and bedded the bottom of our trenches; and when night came on we posted sentries, and huddled down to the bedding. The night was clear, and I gazed unblinkingly at the fierce stars above me, my aching flesh forbidding sleep. Later, I must have dozed in a wakeful stupor.

VIII

The next daybreak, that of the 25th, was less misty. Bread and bully-beef had come up during the night, and we fed to get warmth into our bodies. But the sun was soon up, and we began to feel almost cheerful once again. There was no immediate sign of the enemy, and I walked along to the bridge we had crossed the previous day to glean some information of our intentions; but the only plan seemed to be the obvious one of holding on to our positions. I noticed some engineers were there ready to blow up the bridge if need be.

About 8 A.M. we saw little groups of enemy cavalry appear on the horizon. Through my glasses I could see them consulting maps, pointing, trotting fussily about. Our artillery was planting some kind of scattered barrage on the plain, and an occasional near shot made the horsemen scamper. We watched them rather amusedly till ten o'clock and then we saw signs of infantrymen. They came from the direction of Esmery-Hallon, and at first seemed in fairly dense formation. But they extended as they cut the sky line, and we soon perceived them advancing in open order. As they got nearer, they began to organize short rushes, a section at a time.

We were now well stocked with ammunition—there were piles of it laid about—and as soon as the advancing troops were within anything like range, we began to 'pot' them. In fact, the whole thing became like a rifle-gallery entertainment at a fair. But still they came on. Now we could see them quite plainly—could see their legs working like dancing bears, and their great square packs bobbing up ·and down as they ran. Occasionally one dropped.

Immediately in front of our trench, about eight hundred yards away, there was a little copse of perhaps fifty trees. This they reached about eleven o'clock and halted there. If only our flanks held out, I guessed they would never get farther, for between the copse and our rifles and Lewis guns there was not a shred of cover; and we were well entrenched, with a wide canal in front of us.

Of course, the artillery was busy all the while: not methodically, but thickly enough to give the day the appearance of a conventional battle. But then the unexpected (really we had no cause longer to regard it as unexpected), the fatal thing happened. A battery of ours shortened its range, and got our position exactly 'taped.' The shells fell thick and fast, right into our backs. We were, remember, dug in on the top of a bank, perhaps fifteen feet high. All along this bank the shells plunged. Immediately on our right, not fifty yards away, a shell landed cleanly into a trench, and when the smoke cleared there remained nothing, absolutely nothing distinguishable, where a moment ago had been five or six men. We groveled like frightened, cowed animals. Still the shells fell: and there was no means of stopping them. I glanced distractedly round; men on the right were running under cover of the bank away to the right. Other men on the left were retreating to the left. I resolved to get out of it. Immediately behind us, fifty yards away, was a large crescent-shaped mound, very steep, like a railway embankment, and perhaps sixty feet high. It occurred to me that from there we should command, and command as effectively as ever, the plain in front of us. I made my intention known, and at a given signal we leaped down the bank, and across the intervening fifty yards. We were evidently in sight, for a hail of machine-gun bullets made dusty splutters all round us as we ran. But we reached the mound without a casualty, and climbed safely on to it. There I found a few men already in occupation, commanded by a colonel, under whose orders I then placed myself.

The enemy's artillery fire now increased in volume. I saw a cow hit in a field behind us, and fall funnily with four rigid legs poking up at the sky.

At 3.30 we saw the French retiring on the right, about a thousand yards away. They were not running, but did not seem to be performing any methodic withdrawal. We then fell into one of those awful states of doubt and indecision. What was happening? What should we do? There was angry, ominous rifle-fire on our immediate left. About 4 P.M. there was a burst of machine-gun fire on our immediate right. I noticed that the stray bullets were coming over our heads. This meant that the enemy were advancing from the right.

I then saw English troops withdrawing about six hundred yards away on the right—evidently the troops that had been defending the bridge. I did not hear any explosion, and so far as I know the bridge remained intact.

At 4.15 I saw the colonel with his men suddenly leave his position on my immediate left. Although I was within sight

—within calling distance—he did not give me an order. I was now alone on the mound with my fifteen men.

I did not wait long. I resolved to act on my own initiative once more. We had now moved off the maps I possessed and might as well be in an unknown wilderness. I resolved to proceed due west, taking the sun as a guide. We moved down the back slope of the mound. At the foot we found a stream or off-flow from the canal, about ten feet wide and apparently very deep. As we hesitated, looking for a convenient crossing, a machine-gun a few hundred yards away opened fire on us. There were a good few trees about which must have obstructed the firer's view: the cut twigs, newly budded, fell into the water. We hesitated no longer: we plunged into the stream. The men had to toss their rifles across, many of which landed short and were lost. The sight of these frightened men plunging into the water effected one of those curious stirrings of the memory that call up some vivid scene of childhood: I saw distinctly the water-rats plunging at dusk into the mill-dam at Thornton-le-Dale, where I had lived as a boy of ten.

The water sucked at my clothes as I met it, and filled my field-boots. They seemed weighted with lead now as I walked, and oozed for hours afterwards.

We came out facing a wide plain, climbing gently westward. Machine-gun and rifle-fire still played about us. We could see a church steeple on the horizon due west, and I told the men to scatter and make for that steeple. Shrapnel was bursting in the sky, too high to be effective. We ran a little way, but soon got too tired. A——, a faithful orderly, had stayed with me, and soon we walked over the fields as friends might walk in England. We came across French machine-gunners, who looked at us curiously, asked for news of the situation, but did not seem very perturbed.

We eventually came to the village on the horizon (probably Solente). An officer of the engineers stood by the side of his horse at the cross-roads, smoking a cigarette. He asked me why I was retreating. The question seemed silly: 'We shall have to fight every inch of the way back again,' he said. 'These Frenchmen will never hold them.' I went on, too tired to answer.

Here I saw for the first time a new post stuck on the roadside. It had on it an arrow and 'Stragglers Post' in bold letters. So I was a straggler. I felt very bitter and full of despair.

I followed the road indicated by the arrow. It was dotted with small parties of men, all dejected and weary. We trudged along till we came to the village of Carrepuits. Military police met us at the entrance, and told us to report to the Traffic Control in a house a few hundred yards away. It was now getting dusk. I went into the cottage indicated, and here found an officer, very harassed and bored. Men were collected, and separated into the divisions they belonged to, and then given orders to report to such and such a place. I found a party of about fifty men of my division, and was instructed to take them and report to a divisional headquarters situated in a certain street in Roye.

I've forgotten that walk: it was only about two miles, but our utter dejection induced a kind of unconsciousness in us. It would be between ten and eleven o'clock when we got to Roye. I reported to a staff officer, who sent me off to the town major to get billets. The town major I found distracted, unable to say where I should find a billet. Apparently the town was packed with stragglers. We peered into two great gloomy marquees, floored densely with recumbent men. Meanwhile two other officers joined me with their men, and together we went off to search on our own. We found a magnificent house, quite empty, and here we lodged the men. Some kind of rations had been found. They soon had blazing wood fires going, and seemed happy in a way.

The town major had indicated a hut, where we officers might get rest, and perhaps some food. We went round, tired and aching though we were; we lifted the latch and found ourselves in a glowing room. A stove roared in one corner—and my teeth were chattering with cold, my clothes still being sodden—and a lamp hung from the roof. A large pan of coffee simmered on the stove, and the table was laden with bread, tinned-foods, butter; food, food, food. I hadn't had a bite since early morning, and then not much.

I forget, if I ever knew, who or what the two occupants were, but they were not stragglers. Roye had been their station for some time. One of them was fat, very fat, with a tight, glossy skin. I don't remember the other. We explained that we would like a billet for the night—anything would do so long as it was warmth. They were sorry: they had no room. Could they spare us some rations? They were sorry: this was all they had got till tomorrow noon. We stood very dejected, sick at our reception. 'Come away!' I said. 'Before I go away,' cried one of my companions, 'I would just like to tell these blighters what I think of them.' He cursed them, and then we walked away, back to the men's billet. I looked in at my fellows; most of them were naked, drying their clothes at the fire. Some slept on the floor.

We went upstairs into an empty room. Two of us agreed to make a fire, while the other, the one who had given vent to his feelings, volunteered to go off in search of food. We split up wood we found in the house, and lit a fire. I took off my clothes to dry them, and sat on a bench in my shirt. If I had been asked then what I most desired, besides sleep, I think I would have said: French bread, butter, honey, and hot milky coffee.

The forager soon turned up. God only knows where he got that food from: we did not ask him. But it was French bread, butter, honey, and hot milky coffee in a champagne bottle! We cried out with wonder: we almost wept. We shared the precious stuff out, eating and drinking with inexpressible zest.

As we supped we related our experiences. I forget their names; I don't think I ever knew them. Were they of the Border Regiment? I'm not sure; but they were Northerners. They had been trapped in a sunken road, with a Boche machine-gun at either end, and Boche calling on them to surrender. I don't think either of them was more than twenty years old: they were fresh and boyish, and had been faced with this dilemma. They put it to the vote: there, with death literally staring them in the face, they solemnly called on the men to show hands as to whether they would surrender, or make a run for it. They had voted unanimously for the run. Half of them perished in the attempt. But here, a few hours afterwards, were the survivors, chatting over a blazing wood fire, passing a bottle of coffee round, very unperturbed, not in any way self-conscious. We stacked the fire high and stretched ourselves on the floor in front of it, and slept for a few hours.

IX

We were up at six the next morning, the 26th of March, and reporting to the Assistant Provost-Marshal, who was re-organizing stragglers. We congregated in the Town Square, and I was amazed at the numbers there. The streets were thickly congested with infantrymen from several divisions, with French armored cars, cavalry, and staff officers. We fell in by divisions, and presently marched off, a column a mile or two in length. Cavalry protected our flanks and rear from surprise.

At Villers-les-Roye I found B——, the man who had been separated from me at Ramecourt Bridge. We were glad to be united again, and from there proceeded together. B—— had had orders to go to a place called La Neuville, where the first-line transport awaited us. We were now passing through the battlefields of 1916, and everywhere was desolate and ruined. We marched on as far as Hangest-en-Santerre, where we met our battalion cookers loaded with a welcome meal. Just as we had devoured this, and were starting on our way again, we were met by a staff colonel, who, after in-quiring who we were, ordered us to turn back and proceed to Folies, where our brigade was reorganizing.

We could but mutely obey, but with dull despair and an aching bitterness. We had never thought since leaving Roye but that we were finally out of the melee. To turn back meant, we knew, that we might still be very much in it. We crossed country to Folies, about two miles away, in a blazing sun. There we found the details of the brigade, consisting mostly of returned leave men, already holding a line of trenches. We were told to reinforce them.

Here the second-in-command rejoined the battalion and assumed command. My endurance was broken, and I was ordered down to the transport lines. I pointed out that the men were as weary as I, and should on no account be ordered into action again. It was useless: no man could be spared. But there was not much more for them to bear. Good hot food came up to them again at dusk. The night was warm and restful.

On the morning of the 27th, the enemy had possession of Bouchoir, a village about one mile to the south-east. He began to advance during the morning, and a skirmishing fight went on during that day and the next; and during this time the battalion was withdrawn from the line without suffering any serious casualties.

X

But I had gone back with the transport officer on the 26th. I mounted the transport-sergeant's horse, and in a dazed sort of way galloped westward in the dusk. I arrived half-dead at La Neuville, and slept there for twelve hours or more. The next day we went to Braches, and thence on foot to Rouvrel. About here, the country was yet unscathed by war, and very beautiful. On a bank by the roadside, I took *Walden* out of my pocket, where it had been forgotten since the morning of the 21st, and there began to read it. At Rouvrel the rest of the battalion rejoined us the next day.

On the 29th I set off on horseback with the transport to trek down the valley of the Somme.

When evening came and the hills of Moreuil were faint in the twilight, we were still traveling along the western road. No guns nor any clamor of war could be heard: a great silence filled the cup of misty hills. My weary horse drooped her head as she ambled along, and I, too, was sorrowful. To our north-east lay the squat towers of Amiens, a city in whose defense we had endured hardships until flesh had been defeated, and the brave heart broken. My mind held a vague wonder for her fate—a wonder devoid of hope. I could not believe in the avail of any effort. Then I listened to the rumbling cart, and the quiet voices of the men about me. The first stars were out when we reached Guignemicourt, and there we billeted for the night. In this manner we marched by easy stages down the valley of the Somme, halting finally at Salenelle, a village near Valery, and there we rested four days.

8

THE ARTIST'S DILEMMA

THERE is no book in English literature that I read more often than Coleridge's *Biographia Literaria*. It is not only the source-book and quasi-sacred scripture of that school of literary criticism to which I belong: it is also the intimate confession of one of the most instructive geniuses that ever lived—instructive because so potentially great, so tragically unsuccessful. There is one chapter in this book, the eleventh, to which I have turned again and again, in moments of doubt and when filled with that sense of frustration which affects so many writers today. It is entitled 'An affectionate exhortation to those who in early life feel themselves disposed to become authors,' and there are certain passages in this chapter which have had a quite decisive influence on my life. The following passage in particular haunted me for years:

With the exception of one extraordinary man, I have never known an individual of genius healthy or happy without a *profession,* that is, some *regular* employment, which does not depend on the will of the moment, and which can be carried on so far *mechanically* that an average *quantum* only of health, spirits, and intellectual exertion are requisite to its faithful discharge. Three hours of leisure, unannoyed by any alien anxiety, and looked forward to with delight as a change and recreation, will suffice to realize in literature a larger product of what is truly genial, than weeks of compulsion. Money, and immediate reputation form only an arbitrary and accidental end of literary labour. The hope of increasing them by any given exertion will often prove a stimulant to industry; but the necessity of acquiring them will in all works of genius convert the stimulant into a narcotic.

When I left the Army at the end of January, 1919, I was still uncertain what to do. I had even, for some weeks, considered the possibility of taking a regular commission. My ultimate aim was clear enough: to become an author; and even the Army might be a means to this end. We looked forward then to a long period of peace, and an officer's life in peace-time, I argued, would provide the three hours of leisure which, according to Coleridge, was all I needed. But the more I considered the prospect, the less I liked it. The conditions which had made us 'comrades in arms' would be exchanged for conditions bringing back that world of parade, discipline and snobbery whose fringes I had touched at the beginning of the war, and such a world I could never have tolerated. I soon renounced this possibility, and when I reached London in February of that year, a free man again and a civilian, two careers seemed immediately open to me: politics or the Civil Service.

I did not take long to decide between these alternatives. It is true that I had, in the pre-war period, sometimes thought of a political career, and had become an active speaker in the University Debating Society. But by 1919 my purely literary ambitions were predominant, and I saw no possibility of combining poetry and politics. I therefore decided to enter the Civil Service.

In the Army, as an adjutant, I had already found administrative work to my taste, and even now I take a disinterested pleasure in it. The business of co-ordinating details, presenting summaries, writing minutes and memoranda, though I never saw it as an end in life, never seemed irksome or difficult for me: it was simply part of one's literary aptitude. I was not therefore temperamentally unsuited for the career which opened out to me. Nevertheless, I was profoundly unhappy. I quickly discovered that the Civil Service, and especially a clerkship in the Treasury, was no sinecure. I became a private secretary from that moment and anything like leisure disappeared. It is true that we did not begin work until ten o'clock in the morning, and the lunch hour was often extended to two. But I rarely left the Treasury before half-past six or seven, and by the time I had reached home, for a late dinner, I was tired and exhausted.

The more I contemplated the course ahead of me, the less I liked it. My colleagues around me were for the most part absorbed in their departmental work: it was their main interest, to which they willingly devoted all their energies. But my main interest was outside the service, in the field of literature. I was already associating with the poets and painters whose ideals I shared, and I was actively concerned with the editing of a literary review, *Art and Letters,* which

THE FALCON AND THE DOVE

Frank Rutter and I had founded in 1917* The strain between these two loyalties became intolerable.

* The idea of a monthly review had been first conceived at Leeds before the war. It had originated with Frank Rutter, then director of the City Art Gallery, my friend and mentor in those days. The project was postponed on account of the war, but during 1916 and 1917, in the course of our correspondence, Rutter and I gradually came back to our plan, though in the modified form of a quarterly review. As an officer in the Army I was not able to take any open part in the project, but I was in effect a joint editor, and I contributed to the original cost. Rutter discussed the project with his friends in London and began to gather contributions, which he sent to France for my consideration. The first number was published at the end of June, 1917, in a quarto format of thirty-two pages.

In a prefatory note we made a statement which was unexpectedly topical again twenty-five years later: 'The production of a new Review at the present time seems to call for a word of explanation, though not for apology. . . . Objections on the score of scarcity of paper and shortage of labor may surely be overruled when we remember the reams of paper wasted weekly and the hundreds of compositors daily misemployed on periodicals which give vulgar and illiterate expression to the most vile and debasing sentiments. Friends serving at the Front—some of whom contribute to this first issue—remind us that there are educated men in the Army who would gladly welcome an addition to the small number of publications which appeal to them. Engaged, as their duty bids, on harrowing work of destruction, they exhort their elders at home never to lose sight of the supreme importance of creative art.' The contents which followed were perhaps but a slight substantiation of this aim, but they included drawings by Sickert, Lucien Pissarro, Gilman, Ginner and McKnight Kauffer. The most important article was a survey of the position of painting by Ginner. My own contributions were two poems and a review of James Joyce's *Portrait of the Artist as a Young Man.* Altogether, it was a modest beginning, 'agreeably free,' as the *Times Literary Supplement* noted with relief, 'from extravagance and affectation.' *Art and Letters,* with various changes of editorship, survived until

THE ARTIST'S DILEMMA

Again and again I turned to Coleridge's 'affectionate exhortation,' but presently I could only read it with ironical bitterness. In one passage he addresses his sensible young author in these terms: 'My dear young friend, suppose yourself established in any honourable occupation. From the manufactory or counting-house, from the law-court, or from having visited your last patient, you return at evening,

> Dear tranquil time, when the sweet sense of home
> Is sweetest—

to your family, prepared for its social enjoyments, with the very countenances of your wife and children brightened, and their voice of welcome made doubly welcome, by the knowledge that, as far as *they* are concerned, you have satisfied the demands of the day by the labour of the day. Then, when you retire into your study, in the books on your shelves you revisit so many venerable friends with whom you can converse. Your own spirit scarcely less free from personal anxieties than the great minds, that in those books are still living for you! Even your writing desk with its blank paper and all its other implements will appear as a chain of flowers, capable of linking your feelings as well as your thoughts to events and characters past or to come; not as a chain of iron, which binds you down to think of the future and the remote past by recalling the claims and feelings of the peremptory present.' Dear Coleridge! It is only too plain that from the

---

the spring of 1920. Its contributors included Richard Aldington, Aldous Huxley, Siegfried Sassoon, T. S. Eliot, the three Sitwells, Wyndham Lewis, Ezra Pound, Ronald Firbank, Ivor Richards and Katharine Mansfield.

anxieties of his peremptory present he was looking towards an ideal which only existed in his imagination. For the picture he paints is at best half true. It is true that one returns from the counting-house free from the personal anxieties that beset the professional author; and the sweet sense of home is all the sweeter after a routine day in another atmosphere. But that writing desk with its blank paper and its bright implements (a fountain-pen and a Corona typewriter), inviting as it undoubtedly was, more often than not could only serve as a support for a tired head and an exhausted brain. Nevertheless, to that desk I would tie myself, from ten o'clock to midnight, night after night, year after year, for all the years I remained in the Civil Service. As the products of this self-imposed discipline began to appear in the press and in book-form, people would remark on my industry, even those who did not realize that by far the greater part of my day was spent in another occupation. I do not say this in pride: the experience is only significant because it gives rather a different interpretation to Coleridge's observations. A routine occupation imposes a rhythm on life, if only the repetition of regular hours, regular meals and constant movement. With such a rhythm it is comparatively easy to add, like an additional gear to a machine, a subordinate activity of two hours daily application to a writing-desk. In short, such a life favors productivity of some sort; but it is more than doubtful whether such productivity is more 'truly genial' than the irregular spurts of inspiration upon which a comparatively idle writer will depend. An eye on the clock is already a leakage in the forces of concentration. Neither continuous logical thought

nor long imaginative flights are possible under such conditions. If to one's routine duties one adds a normal measure
of sociability, more than twenty-four hours will often intervene between the periods given over to composition. I have
known days, and sometimes weeks, lie between the beginning and the completion of a sentence!

The first few years, my years at the Treasury, were the
most painful in this respect. My mind was full of projects—
projects for novels, plays and long poems which needed seclusion and ample leisure for their execution. As month after
month went by with nothing accomplished, I worked myself
into a desperate state of dissatisfaction and revolt, until I
came near to resigning my post in the Civil Service in order
to retire to some cottage in the country where I could write
uninterruptedly. But before doing this I took the precaution
to consult two or three of my literary friends who had
already committed themselves in this way and were, in
defiance of Coleridge's advice, pursuing literature as a
trade. By far the most experienced of these was Ford Madox
Ford, whom I had first met in 1918—I had discovered his
name, much to my surprise and delight, in the list of officers
attached to the Tees Garrison, whose staff I had joined in
August or September of that year. Ford was busy trying to
forget that he was a writer, but he welcomed the intrusion
of a young and enthusiastic disciple, and for a few years we
were very good friends. Those few years were the years
during which I still clung to the ambition of being a novelist, and Ford was not unwilling to adopt the role of mentor
—had he not nursed Conrad himself from obscurity to fame!
What confidences I made to Ford I cannot remember; but

I still have a few letters of his, inviting me to come down to Hurston or Bedham, to talk over whatever work was in progress. He preferred to talk, and he was a magnificent talker; but sometimes he would write, and then he was a good letter-writer. The generality of his advice was always the same, and I found it entirely reasonable and sympathetic:

Education Sentimentale is Stonehenge; but What Maisie Knew is certainly Stratford on Avon (though God forbid that the Old Man should hear me say so!). Le Rouge et le Noir is the perfect thing upon which to model one's style, if one does not model it on Coeur Simple—which is worth a wilderness of apes, monkeys, *Times Literary Supplement* Reviewers and almost every other thing in the world. . . . But the Real Thing is nearly as good. Only Henry was just a *little* provincial-pharisaic, whereas Flaubert was so large, untidy, generous—and such a worker! Still, as someone or other said, L'un et L'autre se disent, and if you aren't in the mood for Stonehenge the Birthplace is a very good substitute— and Henry Beyle, perhaps, a better still.

(11:6:20)

If the style of Stendhal was modeled on the Code Napoleon, then mine might have proved not incompatible with the writing of Treasury minutes. It was not the question of style, however, that was worrying me, but the broader problems of composition and execution. 'Broader' problems—I should rather say 'physical' problems. To model myself on Flaubert and Henry James at the fag-end of a busy day in Whitehall—on that physically impossible strain I finally broke.

The dilemma that was forced on me can be stated simply

enough: there was only one kind of fiction I had the conscience to write, and there was no chance of writing it so
long as I stayed in the Civil Service. The fact that I decided
to stay in the Service depended to a considerable degree on
the critical attitude I had adopted to this particular art. This
attitude I owed entirely to Henry James, to whose work I
had first been introduced by Frank Rutter in 1913 or 1914.
Previously I had been, so far as fiction was concerned, almost
completely under the spell of Turgenev and Dostoevsky,
though Meredith, whom I had read in entirety, perhaps prepared me for Henry James. In those days I fancy we regarded Meredith as the immediately preceding stage in the
evolution of the novel—a misunderstanding of essential
values which would have horrified James, whose direct an-
cestry was undoubtedly French. It was from James that I
myself worked back to Maupassant and Flaubert. Between
1914 and 1920 I read practically the whole of James's work,
the greater part of it while I was still in the Army. I became
a fanatical admirer of his art—more particularly of his formal conception of the novel, though at that time I was
equally eager to defend his style and the significance of his
subject-matter. The style was the idiosyncrasy of the man,
and I never had the least temptation to imitate it; and the
subject-matter was, superficially, a social world of which I
had no knowledge. But this social world concealed, beneath
its polished surface, all the moral issues which are the particular concern of the novelist. For me one of James's greatest virtues was that he perceived that the contemporary
scene held all the challenges upon which the dramatic structure of art is built. He did not seek to create a fictitious

world with its faked tragedies and easy feelings. Everything in these novels was real and authentic, and yet out of this genuine material, without the slightest violence or distortion, James made his faultless works of art with their formal relations and figures—elements upon which the profoundest aesthetic emotions depend. It is, as I still believe, an art carried to the pitch of perfection; and the desolating sense that such an art could never be surpassed—could never, without a devotion as long and as severe as his, be equaled—this sense had not a little to do with the decision I took at this time of inner crisis.

Ford, with a persuasive charm that was difficult to resist, threw all his forces on the side of the novel. I still have a long letter which he wrote to me in the September of that fateful year, and I feel no compunction in quoting most of it:

. . . I don't know that I am the most sympathetic person to come to for one inclined to desert the practice of novel writing for the indulgence of metaphysics. For, firstly, I never knew what metaphysics were and, secondly, I have for years and years and years held that the only occupation to which a serious man could seriously put himself was the writing of novels—if only because, in all the varied domains to which the very limited human intelligence applies itself this is the only one that is practically unexplored—the only one in which it is possible to find a New Form. And it is only the finding of a New Form that is a worthy occupation.

So at least I see it—and the immense advantage that the Novel has over the frivolous apparition called the Serious Book —is that, if you are really serious enough you can say what you like. . . . I mean that you can ram all the metaphysics in the world into it and it can still be a fine work of art. . . . Or all the Strategy, Biology, Bibliography and Philately that count.

I don't see what Yorkshire * has to do with it—except that all Yorkshire people, as I have known them, are singularly lazy and singularly self-sufficient (Present Company, of course, always excepted!) My friend Marwood, as you say, was a case in point: he had the clear intelligence of a poet but, rather than trespass on his own shyness and shamefacedness he would spend days making corrections out of his head on the Margins of the *Encyclopaedia Britannica.* He just—peace to his ashes— wanted to bolster up his self-conceit to himself (he didn't boast of the achievement to any other soul), and, of course, to remain très grand seigneur, Marwood of Bushby, and so on. . . . That is at the bottom of most Yorkshire dislike of the Arts—a sort of shyness and love of ease! Your country folk see a Poet performing coram populo! They say to themselves: We dare not appear in public: they say aloud: That is a contemptible fellow! And gradually their public utterance becomes themselves and they end as sidesmen in the local Bethel! And conceal the Venus of Milo, as she used to be concealed in the Leeds Art Gallery, behind aspidistras!

Don't let yourself undergo that hardening process; it is a very stupid one; and try to forget that you come from the Sheeres at all. . . . Whitechapel is really a better lieu de naissance. . . .

Of course I see you aiming at becoming another Henri Beyle: But it is a miserable ambition. . . . Learn of Stendhal all you can—and there is, if you do not happen to be Middleton Murry, an immense deal to learn in an artistic sense. . . . But don't

---

* I fancy it was part of my plan to retreat to Yorkshire and become a regional novelist.

model yourself on him. . . . I can imagine no more terrible being to himself, than a Yorkshireman, true to type, and modeling himself on Mr. Beyle! . . . The end would be the most horribly costive neurastheniac you can imagine, with incredible sex obsessions sedulously concealed, swaddled up to the ears in red flannel for fear of draughts, and with more hypochondrias and phobias than are to be found in all Freud, Jung and the late Marie Bashkirtseff put together. . . . And with a yellow, furred tongue, and a morgue britannique beyond belief. . . .

No, try not to become that. . . . You may not like novel writing but it would be a good thing to stick to it so as to avoid turning your soul into a squirrel in a revolving cage. . . . Still, it is not for me to interfere with the destiny of others and, if you will you will.

Ford treats the problem as one of arbitrary choice: he had an old-fashioned idea of the Civil Service, as an elegant profession for a gentleman, and had no conception at all of the rationalized bureaucratic machine which it had become, within a short time and under the direction of that very department of the Treasury in which I served. As for his warnings about the desiccating effect of metaphysics and psychology, these sprang, not so much from Ford's consideration for me as from his antipathy to any kind of logical thought—even the logic of ordinary consistency in conversation and reminiscence. In this same letter, for example, he writes:

You are unjust, rather, to Conrad. . . . He is a Pole, and, being a Pole is Elizabethan. He has done an immense deal for the Nuvvle in England—not so much as I, no doubt, but then that was not his job, and he is of the generation before mine. I learned all I know of Literature from Conrad—and England has learned all it knows of Literature from me. . . . I do not mean to say that Conrad did not learn a great deal from me when we got going; I dare say he learned more actual stuff of me than I of him. . . . But, but for him, I should have been a continuation of DANTE GABRIEL ROSSETTI— and think of the loss that would have been to you young things. . . . And think what English Literature would be without Conrad and James. . . . There would be nothing!

(19:9:20)

This might be read as humorous bluffing, but not by anyone who knew Ford. He did actually believe that he had been an essential link in the evolution of modern English literature, finding his place somewhere between Conrad and James, but extending past Conrad to 'you young things.' That Conrad owed a lot to Ford, no one who knows the facts can deny; but Conrad owed still more to James himself; and as for James, he had something like pity for the efforts of the 'monstrous Master Mariner,' as he called Conrad; and I suspect that he looked on Ford as one of the young things, and in no sense a coeval.

This falsity in Ford's claim, too obvious to be hidden from even friendly eyes, affected my reception of his advice. I was never actually in any danger of undergoing the hardening process, or of taking Henri Beyle as a model. I did not, that is to say, accept the view that an interest in metaphysics or 'the Serious Book' necessarily meant a loss of humaneness, or even of humor. Ford had such an exclusive feeling for the novel that he was willing to 'ram' anything into it: the form could be inflated until it absorbed the man. My view was rather that the man, the person, came first; and that it was immaterial in what particular form he expressed himself—poem, novel, essay, metaphysics or criticism—so long as he remained true to himself and to his aesthetic principles. The choice of form had to be determined by his circumstances.

Such, at any rate, was my decision. I remained in the Civil Service and my novels remained unfinished or unwritten. I did not dismiss the possibility of returning to the form if at any time I should become free; but I still wonder in what direction the novel can evolve. After Henry James came James Joyce—a stylistic liberation of some significance, but a monument to this same sense of frustration. Is there anything else that comes within comparable range of James? There is an immense amount of clever and condign writing, but compared with the tradition of Flaubert and Henry James, it is either primitive or derivative. Nowhere does the novel exist as a vital art form—as anything but entertainment or reportage (including in this latter term the reportage of the novelist's own ideas and sentiments). It comes nearest to the real thing in certain 'romans policiers'—Simenon in France, Edward Anderson in America, Peter Cheney here, but what a gulf, nevertheless, between *The Golden Bowl* and *Dames Don't Care!*

The decision I had taken meant that such time as I could reserve was to be devoted to the poem and the critical essay. The poem, according to my belief and practice, would come when it would: its generation being a mystery of the unconscious, no precautions that I could take would increase my product by one line. I do not dismiss the possibility of inducing poetic metaphors and images by assiduous exercise: the very act of writing and rhyming is a call-boy to the unconscious. But for such leisurely means I equally had no time. The critical essay is different. One can accumulate notes and ideas over three or four weeks, in trains and buses no less than in the blessed evening hours; and then, when the moment is ripe, a weekend will suffice for the first draft—did suffice for me. Most of my books were built up in this manner, essay by essay. An exception, like *The Green Child*, owes its existence to an unexpected break in the routine; this book I am writing now, to another.

Luckily I have the ability to write without fuss or hesitation, rapidly and enjoyably. I concentrate quickly and in almost any surroundings. Without this faculty, I could not have accomplished half my writings. Indeed, any difficulty in composition would probably have been fatal, for the creative impulse dies if not given a quick chance to materialize, and a continuous sense of frustration is finally too much for the spirit. A sense of frustration was not to be avoided, even in my case; my path is strewn with abandoned projects, with poems damned by not one, but a procession of persons on business from Porlock, with plays which never got beyond the first act and 'ideas for a book' which faded in some attic of the mind. But I have never faltered and never idled, and within certain limits I have written what I wanted to write—not as much as I would like to have written and not necessarily what I would have written for my own pleasure.

The main cause of my frustration was after three years suddenly alleviated. One day, in the normal course of my duties, a letter came up for the signature of the Controller of Establishments which stated that My Lords of the Treasury were pleased to sanction two additional assistant-keeperships in the Victoria and Albert Museum. In a flash I saw a way of escape. If I could be transferred from the Treasury to one of these new posts, then I should be doing work which was not only congenial, but which would surely allow me, far more easily than my duties at the Treasury, to pursue my literary career. I took the letter in for the signature of my chief. As his pen hovered over the sheet of paper, I blurted out my request. The scene that followed was friendly but embarrassing, but my request was granted. With the blessing of the Treasury I went to interview the Director of the Museum, and within a very short time I was appointed to one of the vacancies.

From a worldly point of view my action was irresponsible. I not only sacrificed a considerable part of my income (£150 out of £400), but I threw away one of the most coveted positions in the whole Civil Service. But I have never regretted my action. It is impossible to say what would have happened to me if I had stayed in the Treasury. I might have risen gradually in the hierarchy of that office, or I might have been transferred to some less onerous post in a subordinate department. In any case, the work would not have been congenial, whereas at the Museum I spent ten years full of interest and enlightenment.

I was posted to the Department of Ceramics, a subject about which I then knew nothing. The museums in this country do not normally require any previous expert knowledge as a qualification for a junior post, and though this sometimes shocks our foreign colleagues, who enter their museums armed with doctorates in the history of art, my experience convinces me that the English system is right. A theoretical knowledge is almost entirely irrelevant to the practical work of a museum, and efficiency in theory, which is based on the faculties of memory and reasoning, may give a quite erroneous value to an individual who, in his practical work, must rely on his sensibility and his organizing skill. Sensibility is innate, and it is entirely reasonable that some evidence of possessing this quality should be given by the candidate; it is possible that administrative ability might also be tested in some way. But the real school is the museum itself, and training can only begin with the handling of the actual works of art.

These works, in my case, might not seem to possess much significance in the history of art, and it is, of course, true that the masterpieces of the potter or the glass-blower cannot be compared with those of the painter or sculptor. But I soon discovered that the humblest and least conscious work of art may be more representative of its period than the grandiose masterpiece, which is so often encumbered with irrelevant ideological motives. It depends to a considerable extent on the period. There is practically no aesthetic difference between a Sung vase and a Sung painting; the difference between a maiolica plate and a painting by Piero della Francesca is immense. But even in this Italian example, there is a mutual relationship, and I should suspect a sensibility which made an absolute distinction between them. Certainly no such distinction was made during the Renaissance, and the tradition that Raphael and other masters did not disdain to paint maiolica is only consonant with the whole spirit of the age. In any case, I found the close and systematic study of one branch of art an ideal approach to an understanding of art in general; and ceramics has this unrivaled advantage—its material has rarely suffered by the passage of time: it does not decay or fade, and one has the knowledge that the object presents to its present-day beholder exactly the same basis of sensation that it had for the artist who made it.

Ideal as my new occupation was from the general point of view of interest and congeniality, it had an unsuspected disadvantage from the point of view of an author: it was *too* interesting. It was not a mechanical activity which absorbed only my physical energy and left my mind free. It was in itself a branch of critical activity, and it was quite impossible to make any clear distinction between the work done in official hours and the work done outside. The history and the criticism of art, in which I was involved as part of my duties, merged naturally into the history and criticism of literature, and both took their place in any general conception of culture. It was because I could not make any distinction between these two activities that I inevitably became a critic of art; and since the criticism of art has been relatively neglected in this country since the time of Ruskin, I found plenty to occupy my attention.

The less applied forms of literary activity were bound to suffer, and I was again continually under the necessity of abandoning projects which had no vocational or economic urgency. I still cling to the belief that I was nevertheless expressing myself, and that even art criticism is a literary form. But modern art criticism, which has to abjure the impressionistic graces of a Ruskin or a Pater, which has the historical task of incorporating in art criticism the revolutionary discoveries of anthropology and psychology, must cope with intractable material. Precision and efficiency necessarily take the place, in a modern prose style, of euphony and symphonic rhythm. These new qualities are aesthetic too; but as in modern architecture, the public is slow to recognize them.

I shall describe later the aesthetic philosophy which I gradually evolved as a result of my study of art. That philosophy is an existential one: it is the expression of all my faculties, of the whole consciousness of a living organism; but it was immensely strengthened by this practical application to the material of art. For ten years I was in daily communication with the symbols in which, throughout the centuries, this philosophy has been embodied.

I ended, therefore, by following Coleridge's advice; but Coleridge never followed his own advice and he did not realize the measure of renunciation it entailed. It is perfect advice if a writer is content to express himself in miniscule; but it would not have suited Coleridge's friend Wordsworth —that 'one extraordinary man' he himself excepted—not Milton, nor Shakespeare; for their major effects the whole stage of life had to be cleared of impedimenta, even impedimenta domestica.

This last phrase suggests that I have avoided one of the issues. Coleridge, with Christian largess, assumes that the writer has a family. It is true that the crisis which I faced, and which every writer without independent means has to face, is considerably reduced in acuteness if marriage and its consequences are renounced. The artist, if he is to devote himself entirely to his art, should be celibate; not only celibate, but monastic. The lives of most artists who have married end in tragedy or bitterness; but the lives of the unmarried artists are not noticeably happier. If we take the two extremes of Tolstoy and Baudelaire—one almost patriarchal and the other Ishmaelish—they will be found to produce, by different means, the same miseries. Indeed, the problem of celibacy or marriage, of life with women or life without them, is probably quite subordinate, or at most contributory, to the fundamental problem. There is in the artist a psychological condition which is favorable to the functioning of the creative imagination: it is a certain condition of dialectical stress or tension. Such a condition is not likely to arise from a life of placid contentment. The greatest enemy of art is, alas, happiness. I do not know enough about the lives of great composers; but I can think of no great poet or painter whose life can be described as predominantly happy. If they achieve happiness at some stage, it will be found that the works of art they then produce could not have existed without a precedent period of stress; that actually their best work is a direct product of such periods. Naturally, by stress I do not necessarily mean a condition of open distress: the tension, that is to say, may be hidden in the unconscious.

From a vague awareness of this truth, a wrong conclusion is sometimes reached about the relations of the artist to society. It is pointed out that some of the most artistically productive periods in history—the Renaissance in Italy, the

Elizabethan period in England—have been periods of war, tyranny or social unrest. It is true that such social conditions may affect the life and happiness of the individual artist; but it is false logic to assume that they are the only or a necessary cause of cultural activity. The relation of the artist to society, and of culture to civilization, is extremely complicated. It is probably much more a question of mental reactions to moral and psychological pressures and releases than of any external conflict. The artist himself prefers peace: peace which allows him to concentrate his powers and hold his audience. There are enough wars within his own mind to occupy his attention; and the dialectical contradiction between this inner stress and an outward calm is probably the condition most favorable to the creative impulses. A study of English literature between 1815 and 1915 would support this view.

To return to my subject: the marriage of a poet cannot be judged by the plus or minus of happiness which it brings, because happiness is inessential. What is far more important is that the poet should experience certain depths of feeling in the natural man which can only come from marriage and parentage. However vicarious the imagination, in its external visitations, it can never recover the elemental emotions which are those of the husband and wife, the father and mother. And what have these elemental emotions to do with the nature of art? Only this: before there can be art there must, as Rilke said, be memories, and before there can be memories there must be experiences. It is not so much on the variety of experience that the poet depends, but on certain essential experiences which have depths: the innocent eye of childhood, the blurred ecstasies of adolescence, the intense joy of love, the shock of death; and to these I would add the experience of marriage.

Each artist must find an individual solution of the dilemma which is implicit in his acceptance of society. To a few who are favored by tradition and wealth the solution may come easily; they have probably nothing to fear but the uneasy conscience of the rentier and the envy of their colleagues. But for most artists some form of sacrifice or renunciation is involved: they must surrender their isolation; they must subordinate their artistic ideals to the baser demands of entertainment. Or they may prefer to keep their ideals and curtail their ambitions. But this alternative is apt to bring with it an occasional bitterness of the spirit. One willingly throws ballast overboard so long as it consists of replaceable things; but when we come to the children of our imagination, then the hand is reluctant.

9

PROFITABLE WONDERS

THIS story of the awakening of my mind has reached a point at which I can conveniently break it off; the story is not finished, nor, I hope, will it ever be finished so long as I retain the faculties of perception and reasoning. But before I bring the narrative to an end with some kind of retrospective summary, there are certain influences which ought to be acknowledged. They had not been mentioned before, either because they are the kind of influences which any educated man may be assumed to have undergone, or because they are influences which have been so completely absorbed that, like mother's milk, they have been forgotten. There may be still others which one would like to forget because they have been outgrown and discarded. These, too, should be recorded.

Among the influences which are not only assumed, but absorbed to the point of being no longer conscious, are the English Bible and Shakespeare. I am glad that I was born soon enough to be brought up as a matter of course on the Bible. It was given to us as scripture, but we absorbed it, unconsciously, as art; and it stands in almost the same relation to English prose as Shakespeare does to our poetry. I say 'almost' because, in the first place, 'the voice that roars along the bed of Jewish song' is not a prosaic voice, even in our translation. This is not the place for observations on the nature of English prose style—I have made them elsewhere; but from the Bible there derives one special kind of exalted prose—the prose of Taylor, Browne and Ruskin—which is far removed from the functional prose of Swift and Maine. But this exaltation, oriental or Hebraic in its source, is crystallized in the primitive grandeur of the Authorized Version, and thence infuses the imaginative genius of our race. An exotic element, it is not the less evident, for those who have ears to hear, than the visible traces of Syrian and Byzantine are which lie scattered across our country, even as far as the wastes of Northumbria and the Hebrides.

I do not wish to imply that the English Bible should be treated only as a literary document; nor that its influence on me was entirely, or even predominantly, artistic. Nevertheless, the effect of the Bible in itself is not in any profound sense religious: it is an epic story and not a manual of devotion. But as an epic, a religious epic, it is what we call in our poor critical jargon 'a human document.' Such episodes as the legend of Joseph, the trial of Job, and scores of others, not to mention the Passion of Jesus, work upon the primary emotions and make us acquainted with the full pathos and tragic significance of our human destiny. When all religions have passed, or become transformed, or merged, this book will still remain as the Bible of Mankind.

I cannot claim, like some people, to have lived continuously with Shakespeare's works. He is, for me, the greatest of the romantic poets, and the justification for all time of the romantic theory of art. For that reason alone he occupies an essential place in my intellectual world. But perhaps just because he is so completely romantic, he is so didactically negative. Not even the German critics have been able to reconstruct Shakespeare's 'Weltanschauung.' We can find in Shakespeare half-a-dozen separate philosophies of life, according to the mood and predilection with which we read him. It is true that there is what has been called an 'essential' Shakespeare, but there is no clue to it except what another poet can provide by his sympathy and intuition. Shakespeare was everyman—that is an acceptable commonplace. But the capacity to be everyman—that is only given to the poet, and it is only in so far as one has felt the poetic ecstasy in one's self that one has penetrated to any idea of the essential Shakespeare.

Shakespeare has been for me, therefore, the essential poet, 'self-school'd, self-scann'd, self-honor'd, self-secure.' I have turned to him whenever I wished to renew my sense of what was primordial in the nature of the poet. He would not, of course, have held this peculiar position in my regard, and in the regard of all romantics, if he had not been the supreme English poet—supreme, I mean, in the actual texture of his verse. It is possible to argue about Shakespeare's philosophy, or his dramatic structure, or even about his identity; but the verbal beauty of his language is unquestionably supreme. The only question is whether this supremacy, this 'loftiest hill' which

> Spares but the cloudy border of his base
> To the foil'd searching of mortality,

has not so dominated English poetry that it has acted as an inhibition. The seventeenth century, which was too near to him, and the eighteenth which ignored him, escaped the dilemma; but from the time of the Romantic revival every poet has had to contend with Shakespeare's stylistic influence, and submit to it or flee from it. The trouble is that Shakespeare's poetic diction is such a quintessence of the English language, that the poet can only escape from it into artificialities—the artificiality of Milton's latinity, of Wordsworth's 'common speech,' of Browning's elliptic harshness. On the whole, it is better to acknowledge and accept his supremacy, as Keats and Shelley and Tennyson did: in that way there are variations to be won. The only honest alternative is one which has been attempted by several poets of our own generation: to base poetry on visual rather than verbal appeal.

Others have written so fully on Shakespeare and the Bible that there is nothing new to say at this late day. The best tribute to the Bible is Ruskin's, who was himself obsessed by this influence; and it is to Ruskin that I would now like to pay my tribute. When I first began to read Ruskin, about 1909 or 1910, his tradition was still alive. There were still many people who had known him personally, who were in effect his disciples, and who regarded him as a seer and a prophet. This Ruskin fellowship had inevitably created a reaction, and a slump in his reputation set in. The second-hand bookshops were flooded with his works, and one could pick up excellent editions at sixpence or a shilling a volume. There is still, I believe, a Ruskin Society, but though some faithful followers survive among our septa- and octogenarians, his readers must now be few, and his influence practically extinct. It is, I am convinced, a temporary eclipse. He presents two aspects for our continued consideration: his thought and his style; and it is of his style that I am most confident. It has a wide range, from exact objective description to the emotive evocation of beauty and pathos, and it is always superb. It was another great prose artist, in another language, who was to pay this style the highest tribute—the tribute of transplantation. Marcel Proust applies the style to a very different material, but though it then strikes such an individual note in French literature, it is very familiar to anyone accustomed to the rhythms of Ruskin's style. What is surprising about this style is not its simplicity, which one might have expected from a man so obsessed with the English Bible, but its variety and complexity, its intellectual control of the sensuous verbal elements. A sentence like the following, necessarily long, has the elaborate phrasing of a musical cadenza:

Every blade of grass burned like the golden floor of heaven, opening in sudden gleams as the foliage broke and closed above it, as sheet-lightning opens in a cloud at sunset; the motionless masses of dark rock—dark though flushed with scarlet lichen, casting their quiet shadows across its restless radiance, the fountain underneath them filling its marble hollow with blue mist and fitful sound; and over all the multitudinous bars of amber and rose, the sacred clouds that have no darkness, and only exist to illumine, were seen in fathomless intervals between the solemn and orbed repose of the stone pines, passing to lose themselves in the last, white, blinding lustre of the measureless line where the Campagna melted into the blaze of the sea.

THE FALCON AND THE DOVE

An age devoted to functional values cannot appreciate such prose; but there is more than one kind of prose, and not to respond to Ruskin betrays a sensibility as limited as that of the modern dilettante who cannot enjoy the paintings of Poussin or Claude—or those of Turner, to give a more exact parallel. But to appreciate the range of Ruskin's style, a passage of the kind I have quoted should be compared with the invective of *Fors Clavigera* or the simple 'talk' of *Praeterita*. It may be that Ruskin himself despised his artistic genius ('I don't care whether you have enjoyed them (his books) or not. Have they done you any good?') and at one time he was cynical enough to use his evocative powers as so much stylistic gilding for the ethical pill: he deliberately went over some of his books and worked in purple passages to make them more attractive to the public. But Ruskin is not the first nor the last artist to despise (or fear) his artistic powers; the main thing is that he used them, and that by the exercise of a little patience we can still read with enjoyment what he wrote with inspiration.

The patience is necessary, not merely because Ruskin is an irregular and rambling writer, but also because his ideas are a mass of contradictions, perversities, irrelevancies and truths. I shall not refer to his ethical nor (what almost comes to the same thing) his economic ideas, though these are by no means out of date or visionary; for by the time I had reached Ruskin I had also reached Morris and Marx, Kropotkin and Carpenter, and their political writings made more impression upon me because they were more rational and more realistic. But Ruskin's writings on art were a different matter. Before I could read German (which I learned between 1922 and 1925) Ruskin, with the exception of Baudelaire, was the only critic of art that I could at once read and respect. People still do not realize how primitive the criticism of art is in this country—not merely as a science, which it can never, strictly speaking, become, but as a logical activity. Art as a mode of knowledge with its own epistemology of art which must precede any philosophy of art—all these are aspects of the subject which were unknown, unthought of, at the time of Ruskin's death. But when Ruskin himself first approached the subject, the situation was infinitely worse: art criticism was nothing but descriptive impressionism; and impressionism is too flattering a word for what was little more than an account of the sentimental associations aroused by a work of art. There had been a certain amount of philosophical generalization about art—the best of it, represented by Reynolds, being tempered by practical commonsense; but Ruskin was the first critic to insist on a definition, not merely of philosophical terms like 'truth' and 'beauty,' but of psychological concepts like 'color,' 'space,' 'imagination,' and 'expression'; and he made some attempt to relate the aesthetic activity to life as a whole. Ruskin did not evolve any comprehensive or coherent theory of art; and he is usually treated with contempt by modern aestheticians. But if one is not a system-maker; if one seeks for truth of perception rather than logical coherence, then there is more to be learned from Ruskin than from any previous writer on the subject, with the possible exception of Hegel; and it is not until we come to Nietzsche, Croce and Bergson that we once again pick up the threads of vital thought. Croce would rather trace his affinities to Vico, Hegel and De Sanctis; but for all his contempt of Ruskin, it is Ruskin's theory of expression, his theory of art as language, that come nearer to Croce's aesthetic than any preceding treatment of the subject.

If we turn from theory to historical interpretation, the greatness of Ruskin is all the more apparent. The Gothic Revival was almost a spent force when Ruskin began to publish *The Stones of Venice* in 1851 (it was unfortunately to continue as an ecclesiastical habit); but that Revival had been largely an artificial taste, a sophisticated reaction to an equally artificial classicism. It was Ruskin who first got under the stones and revealed the spirit of Gothic, who first interpreted the social economy of the Middle Ages in the terms of this spirit, and who analyzed the characteristics of the art which expressed this spirit. His famous chapter on 'The Nature of Gothic' still remains a masterpiece of generalization based on the exact knowledge of particulars—the greatest essay in art criticism in our language. Nearly a hundred years have elapsed since Ruskin studied this subject, and we now have a much greater fund of historical and archaeological facts; but in all these years we have not advanced on Ruskin's love and understanding of the art which, for two or three brief centuries, was the supreme expression of the transcendental value of the northern races. If we ever recover our sense of these values—and we must recover them if we are to produce another great art style— we shall return to Ruskin for inspiration and guidance.

William Morris, whose name I have mentioned and would like to mention again, came as an appendix to Ruskin. A disciple of Ruskin's, he had qualities which made him in many ways a more sympathetic figure; but these were qualities of his personality rather than of his writing: his robustness, directness, and practical energy. Though in my youth I read *News from Nowhere* and *The Dream of John Ball* with enthusiasm, and though I have always felt that Morris is a valuable connecting link between art and socialism, his predominant ideas have been a hindrance rather than a help. He can confess on one and the same page his hatred of modern civilization and his inability to read economics. His 'practical' socialism was only possible as an ideal because he ignored the major problems of the age: the problems created by the growth of populations and the development of mass production; the disequilibrium due to the uneven distribution of natural resources; and many other related factors. His ideals were retrospective: he had tried to read Marx, but he did not realize that the process of history is always dialectical—a synthetic leap forward from existing contradictions—and that we must not scrap our machinery, but perfect and control it; we must not assume that art and machinery are mutually exclusive, but experiment until we discover a machine art. Always we must go forward with the instruments which evolution or invention has placed in our hands, and if we have intelligence enough to establish our principles and sensibility enough to express them, then a new art will develop in a new world. We have now lived long enough to be aware of the first signs of such an art.

The theoretical interest in art first aroused in me by Ruskin and Morris eventually led by devious paths to Croce's *Aesthetic,* and from that book, aided by its historical survey of the subject, I branched off into an exploration of a whole province of human thought—a province remarkable for its wastes and scrub rather than for any fertile ground. Croce's book was an essential stage in my development, but I never became a Crocean—some innate empiricism left me indifferent or uncomprehending before his idealism. The more I tended to accept his intuitional theory of art, the more baffled I became by his critical judgments, which seemed to proceed from a narrow classicism and even from a moral priggishness; until I concluded that he had always been a victim of his own environment. But Bergson, to whom I inevitably came, was much more to my taste, and his *Creative Evolution* is certainly one of the books which have had a decisive influence, not merely on the direction of my intellectual growth, but also on its quality. Like most people, I was to outgrow Bergson (though never to become entirely faithless), but when I read him at the age of twenty-five, it was with a passionate absorption which I was never to recover, never to devote to any other philosopher. The explanation is probably simple. The loss of religious faith, which I have described in an earlier chapter, had left me with little more than a mechanistic interpretation of the universe—a bleak rationalism which was not consistent with my romantic temperament. Bergson, keeping within the world of scientific fact—indeed, drawing all his evidence from that world—offered an interpretation of the universe which was neither mechanistic nor finalist—which provided a way out of the closed system of predestined fact. He showed that the system contains a principle of change: that simply to exist is to change: that to change is to mature, and that to mature is to create ever new elements in the universe.

He gave validity to such terms as consciousness and intuition
—terms upon which, I already then perceived, any philosophy of art must rely. (I should perhaps say any philosophy
of romanticism, but that is a distinction which, as I shall
presently suggest, makes no difference.) 'Art lives on creation and implies a latent belief in the spontaneity of nature.'
Sentences like this showed that Bergson himself was aware
that art had some evidence to offer for his theory; and when
he comes to define intuition, by which he means 'instinct
that has become disinterested, self-conscious, capable of reflecting upon its object and of enlarging it indefinitely,' he
uses the aesthetic faculty as a proof that such a process is
possible. 'Our eye perceives the features of the living being,
merely as assembled, not as mutually organized. The intention of life, the simple movement that runs through the
lines, that binds them together and gives them significance,
escapes it. This intention is just what the artist tries to re-
gain, in placing himself back within the object by a kind of
sympathy, in breaking down, by an effort of intuition, the
barrier that space puts up between him and his model.' *

Passages like this in *Creative Evolution* and in other works
of Bergson's made me wish that he would one day give us
his own Aesthetic, but though he continued to throw intermittent lights on the subject, especially in his *Deux sources
de la morale et de la religion,* that desired work remained
unwritten, and is now past hoping for. Perhaps it would not
have been adequate: the material upon which any satisfactory aesthetic should be based has, with recent advances

* Translated by Arthur Mitchell, Ph.D. (London: Macmillan,
1914.)

in anthropology and psychology, become extremely complex, and it will need a youthful energy to cope with it. Not that Bergson's mind was clouded in his later years. The book which I have just mentioned, which was published in 1932, is still as clear and as profound as the great works which made his reputation. The tide of fashion has receded from this figure; but whatever new idols have found (A. N. Whitehead, Karl Barth, John Dewey) seem to me to owe something to Bergson.

I fancy that the rise of Freud's influence has had a good deal to do with the decline of Bergson's. Not that they are at all comparable—one is a metaphysician using scientific material, the other a scientist who occasionally trespasses, not always successfully, into metaphysics. But Freud's hypothesis of the unconscious, a hypothesis which he has established by scientific method and demonstrated by therapeutic practice, is so revolutionary in its implications that it makes a revision of our philosophical and moral concepts a first necessity, and that revision affects the very terms, such as consciousness and instinct, upon which Bergson's metaphysical structure depends. I began to read Freud as soon as the translations of his works appeared in this country, and it at once became evident to me that my own particular sphere of aesthetic criticism would henceforth have to revolve on a new axis. The extent to which I was alarmed may be judged from an article on 'Psycho-analysis and the Critic' which appeared in the *Criterion* in January, 1925; and my *Collected Essays* show, for anyone who has the interest to trace their chronological development, the increasing influence of Freud's psychology upon my critical method.

Even before I read Freud, I tended to probe beneath the
surface of the work of art, my conviction being that the work
of art is either an objective phenomenon which we accept
integrally and sensuously and therefore without intellectual
understanding; or that alternatively it demands for its understanding, not merely a measured view of its external
aspects, but also a complete analysis of the circumstances in
which it came into existence. This latter type of criticism I
have called genetic, and it may, if so desired, be separated
from aesthetic criticism. But an adequate criticism must include both methods, for we must understand, not only form,
rhythm, harmony, composition, texture, handling, etc., but
also imagery, allegory, analogy, motivation, social significance, and many other aspects of the work of art to which
psychology alone can offer the right approach.

I shall not say anything more about Freud's influence,
because it is still active, and psycho-analysis itself is by no
means a subject which can yet be clearly focused. I have
used Freud's name too exclusively: I prefer his method and
his general outlook, but I am not an uncritical disciple. I
believe that Roland Dalbiez has given a fair and objective
estimate of his position in *La méthode psychoanalytique et
la doctrine Freudienne;* and I believe that some of Freud's
errant disciples, particularly Jung and Trigant Burrow, are
nearer than their master to certain aspects of the truth.

I began these random notes with the English Bible and
have ended with Freud. Influences should by nature be
solemn and impressive; it is only when we come to speak of
preferences that we can bring forward minor figures. Many
of my preferences should by now be obvious. Books that

have influenced us, even decisively, may now gather dust on our shelves, as Croce's and Bergson's do on mine. But our preferences are in continual use, a bright part of our equipment. I confess that there are very few books which come into this category in my case. I have already spoken of some of my favorite poets: I return to Donne, Blake, Coleridge and Hopkins most frequently, and never tire of them. Shelley and Whitman I read at longer intervals, but then fairly intensively; and Shakespeare himself comes into this division. I have refrained from speaking of Wordsworth, partly because I have written a separate book about him, partly because he is a little too near to me. We both spring from the same yeoman stock of the Yorkshire dales, and I think I have a certain 'empathetic' understanding of his personality which gives a sense of betrayal to anything I write about him. If I do not write more fully about him now, it is not because I forget how much his poetry has meant to me.

It would be vain and superfluous to pass in review all the poets whose work has, at some time or other, stirred my imagination, or even to trace the mutations of their appeal. But there is one type of book which is perhaps exceptional. It is not easy to classify, but somewhere within its shifting outlines it includes a prose-form which, in the sense that I would most like to imitate it, I most admire. It is represented by Sterne's *Sentimental Journey* and De Vigny's *Servitude et Grandeur militaires;* Merimée's *Carmen* and De la Motte-Fouqué's *Undine;* Mörike's *Mozart auf der Reise nach Prag* and Jacobsen's *Niels Lynne.* Usually it has an historical incident or episode as its basis, but it may be a pure fantasy, like Alain-Fournier's *Le grand Meaulnes*. It is short, it is deliberate; at once realistic and imaginative, objective and reflective. It avoids the psychological approach of the novel and is more than a short story. When it has a moral or satirical motive, like Voltaire's *Candide,* it is sometimes called the *conte philosophique.* The philosophy, however, is best left to the inference of the reader.

Such writings are not constructive art forms: they have neither the organization of the novel nor the simple unity of the short story. They are rather projections of an idea, of an incident, of a fantasy; intellectually conceived, but exhibiting the fresh texture of a personal style and the brightness of a concrete imagination. It is impossible to justify my preference for this genre on any theoretical grounds: I fancy that it is determined simply by the material conditions which make it the form most easily within my grasp, both as a reader and as a writer. Certainly it is not that the informality of such writings is in itself a romantic preference: romanticism is not essentially a formal question, but something much more profound. I shall explain the distinction in more philosophical terms in the next part of this book; here I would only point out that among my strongest personal preferences are poets like Arnold and Hopkins, novelists like Flaubert and Henry James, and painters like Poussin and Seurat, in all of whom formality is almost an obsession. The constructive movement in modern architecture, sculpture and painting is again of a formal purity not excelled in any classical period; and yet it is an essentially romantic art, or I would not have spent so much of my energy in its defense. Le Corbusier, Brancusi, and Ben Nicholson are romantic

THE FALCON AND THE DOVE

artists; but I would make the same claim for Luciano di Laurana, Bernini, and Piero della Francesca. Romanticism and classicism are defined, neither by a period nor a style, but by a psychological attitude to the process of artistic creation—on the one side inspiration, daring and originality; on the other, derivation, conformity and timidity.

PART III

THE
ADAMANTINE SICKLE

And having received also from Hermes an adamantine sickle he flew to the ocean and caught the Gorgons asleep.

APOLLODORUS, II, iv. 2.

THE ADAMANTINE SICKLE

THE reader who has followed my narrative thus far will perhaps have been left with the impression that I have taken him to three or four halting-places and given no hint of a final destination. More than once I have emphasized the fact that I do not consider even the ordinary process of education at an end; my intellectual curiosity is, indeed, insatiable. But the mere acquisition of knowledge has never been my aim—otherwise I could so easily have become an academic scholar or an archaeologist. I am only interested in facts that feed an interest which is total, directed to the universe and to life as an existing whole; and it is my intuition of the nature of that wholeness, my desire to hold it within my mind as a coherent conception, which drives me on to the discovery of facts and their reconciliation in a philosophy of life. In a sense I am a solipsist: that is to say, I believe that the world I discover, as well as the philosophical interpretation I give to it, is contained within myself, and inevitably conditioned by my temperament. Nietzsche's command: Become what thou art, seems to me to be an improvement even on the Delphic oracle. Thus, so long as I remain true to that command, I find myself continually returning to certain fundamental beliefs or attitudes which have their unity or reconciliation in my personality. In this Part I shall try to describe them.

If I begin with aesthetics, it is because I have accumulated most evidence of this kind, and found it a sufficient basis for a general philosophy. I do my ideas too much honor by calling them a philosophy, and it seems doubtful if I shall ever have the time or leisure to elaborate them even into the outline of a philosophical system. But such as they are, these ideas are universal in their implications, and referable to other lives than mine.

My profoundest experience has been, not religious, nor moral, but aesthetic: certain moments of creative activity and, less intense but more frequent, certain moments of sensibility in the presence of works of art. The very vividness of this kind of experience led me to wonder about its nature and to inquire into its place in the universal scheme of things. It gradually became clear to me that the aesthetic experience was not a superficial phenomenon, an expression of surplus energy, a secondary feature of any kind, but rather something related to the very structure of the universe. The more we analyze a work of art, whether it be architecture, painting, poetry or music, the more evident it becomes that it has an underlying structure; and when reduced to abstract terms, the laws of such a structure are the same whatever the kind of art—so that terms such as 'rhythm,' 'balance' and 'proportion' can be used interchangeably in all the arts.

It was a short and obvious step to recognize at least an analogy and possibly some more direct relation, between such a morphology of art and the morphology of nature. I began to seek for more exact correspondences, first by making myself familiar with the conclusions reached by modern physicists about the structure of matter, and then by exploring the quite extensive literature on the morphology of art. Certain correspondences are easily established—the prevalence, for example, in art and in both organic and inorganic matter of the proportion known as the Golden Section. In the course of my research I naturally came across D'Arcy Thompson's *Growth and Form,* and this book, by showing that certain fundamental physical laws determine even the apparently irregular forms assumed by organic growth, enormously extended the analogy between art and nature. All this was a question of exact measurements and demonstrable equations, and merely gave a contemporary scientific sanction to the intuitions of Pythagoras and Plato, who centuries ago had found in *number* the clue to both the nature of the universe and the definition of beauty. Modern physicists, I found, might express themselves much more obscurely, but their implications were the same. In 1922 I found every confirmation I needed in Whitehead's *Principles of Natural Knowledge,* and I noted with zeal passages such as the following: 'Life is complex in its expression, involving more than percipience, namely desire, emotion, will, and feeling. It exhibits variations of grade, higher and lower, such that the higher grade presupposes the lower for its very existence. *This suggests a closer identification of rhythm as the causal counterpart of life; namely, that wherever there is some rhythm there is some life, only perceptible to us when the analogies are sufficiently close.* The rhythm is then the life, in the sense in which it can be said to be included within nature.' There are other passages in this book which might, without any violence, be transposed from a work on physics to one on aesthetics. Here is one more example: 'A rhythm involves a pattern and to that extent is always self-identical. But no rhythm can be a mere pattern; for the rhythmic quality depends equally upon the differences involved in each exhibition of the pattern. The essence of rhythm is the fusion of sameness and novelty; so that the whole never loses the essential unity of the pattern, while the parts exhibit the contrast arising from the novelty of their detail. A mere recurrence kills rhythm as surely as does a mere confusion of differences. A crystal lacks rhythm from excess of pattern, while a fog is unrhythmic in that it exhibits a patternless confusion of detail.'

The analogy, particularly with the qualification implied in this second passage quoted from Whitehead, would account for the formal appeal of a large part of the world's art. But the more I thought of it, the more I became convinced that it would not include everything; and the part that was excluded was the part in which I was especially interested—romantic art. At one time I was tempted to find the distinction between classic and romantic art precisely in this difference: that the one observed the formal laws inherent in the structure of nature, while the other ignored them for the sake of some other values. But I think it has now been convincingly demonstrated (at least, in such test cases as the Parthenon) that even in its most pure and formal manifestations, classic art intuitively avoids an *exact* observation of the laws of natural morphology. It comes every near to them, and then, as if to assert the freedom of the artist's will, narrowly avoids them.

In romantic art, however, there is no such flirtation. Certain laws, of proportion and rhythm, are observed in all but the most anarchic types of expressionism; but having gone so far on the basis of such laws, the work of art then seems to take a leap into the unknown. The laws themselves are contradicted, or are entirely disregarded; and a new reality is created, requiring a sudden passage from perception to intuition, and carrying with it a heightened mode of consciousness.

The analogy for this transition was ready waiting in the new quantum theory. But to pursue this analogy, even granted that the quantum theory itself had been definitely established, would have been too delicate and difficult a task. I was content with the fact that physics had apparently provided an escape from a situation that threatened to be wholly mechanistic. If all art could be referred to natural laws, to a system of numerical proportions, then evidently we were within reach of tests and measurements—in short, of academic rules which meant an end to all creative originality (in the Bergsonian sense) and therefore to all artistic evolution. But though physics might still have its problems to solve, and though the universe was far from being mapped out in its entirety, my analogical excursions had convinced me that a profound relation exists between the reality of art and the reality of nature—a conviction which Whitehead, approaching from the opposite direction, had also reached.

In short, the aesthetic view of life, which Kierkegaard had

perceived as a possibility, had become much more realistic and practical, and I began to consider how far it would carry one in the conduct of life.

In the sphere of morals there did not seem to be any difficulty. Having rejected any code of morality dependent on a supernatural sanction, the only alternatives seemed to be, either an egoism as extreme as Max Stirner's, or a social code determined by the needs and guaranteed by the laws of the community of which one was a member. This latter solution was too relative and too pragmatic for my taste; and fundamentally I had no belief in social sanctions of any kind—they are only an excuse for tyranny. I therefore fell back upon some form of egoism, but though I recognized the logicality of the extremist position, and its freedom (Stirner took his motto from Goethe: 'Ich hab' mein' Sach' auf Nichts gestellt'), I was not prepared for its consequences, which seemed to me to involve hedonism (a life of unrestricted sensuousness, which always ends in despair) rather than a desirable eudemonism (a life of ordered goodness). But it gradually occurred to me that the principles I was working out in the aesthetic sphere could, as Plato had already suggested, be carried over into the ethical sphere, and that a valid analogy existed between the order of the universe, the order of art and the order of conduct. Goodness is living beauty—life ordered on the same principles of rhythm and harmony that are implicit in a work of art. Vulgarity is the only sin, in life as in art. The only danger of such a code was that it might lead to a priggish conformity or preciousness; but here again the analogy of the quantum theory came to my aid. At certain moments the individual is carried beyond his rational self, onto another ethical plane, where his actions are judged by new standards. The impulse which moves him to irrational action I have called the sense of glory, a phrase which is sometimes misunderstood, but which I find too appropriate to abandon. Related to this concept of glory is the concept of honor, which is the personal aspect of the sense of glory and a modest restraint on its expression—'L'honneur, c'est la pudeur virile,' wrote De Vigny. No considerations of utility or expediency can explain the actions of men who at the inspired moment will throw away life itself to achieve their glory or to safeguard their honor; but without these concepts, life is reduced to a routine and cautious existence only worthy of meaner animals.

Admittedly such a morality has its dangers, and may be used in self-justification by any lunatic with a lust for power. But lunatics are a product of a diseased society, and I do not accept the gloomy doctrine that society is necessarily diseased. The impulse to depart from normal standards of the good and the beautiful usually arises from the felt need of new and higher standards. If it is asked who is to be a judge of this need, then the answer is: the artist—the artist in that broad but special sense which includes all men who are capable of acts of creative originality, of instants of intuitive understanding of the nature of reality. An artist in relation to morals is more commonly known as a mystic, and it is sometimes very difficult to say where the poet ends and the mystic begins (I have already mentioned St. Theresa and St. John of the Cross, and Blake is the best English example).

To what extent these doctrines are supported by modern psychology is perhaps a matter of opinion: to some extent it will depend on the interpretation we give to the findings of that science. But the moment of creative inspiration, whether it takes place on the plane of ethics or of art, is dynamic: it is caused by the sudden release of some kind of energy, and the only energy in question is psychic energy. I have put forward my own hypothesis in *Art and Society* (Chapter 5), and it fits in with Freud's anatomy of the mental personality. It is only necessary to say here that this hypothesis accounts, not merely for the source of the energy underlying the phenomenon of inspiration, but also for the formal unity and ideological significance which is given to the verbal or plastic expression of an inspiration.

It is on the basis of this philosophy of art that I have given my support to that movement in contemporary art known as Surrealism. Some of my friends and critics, recognizing the reasonableness of my general attitude, have accused me of inconsistency—of 'flirting with the disreputable muse of Surrealism.' Whether what I mean by Surrealism corresponds to what that word means to its foremost French exponents is perhaps not certain: my interpretation is probably much wider. I have always regarded Surrealism as a first step towards a revindication and re-integration of the romantic tradition. Surrealism has developed various experimental methods: automatic writing, psychopathic simulation, 'paranoiac criticism'; but the means must not be confused with the end, which is nothing less than the application of the dialectical method to the problems of art, leading to a new synthesis of reality and unreality, of reason and unreason, of reflection and impulse. The laws which govern material reality, and which are the conscious or unconscious basis of a rational art, only carry us to the threshold of another order of reality, to which the dream is our main clue. 'It is only at the approach of the fantastic,' André Breton has said, 'at a point where human reason loses its control, that the most profound emotion of the individual has the fullest opportunity to express itself.' More than two thousand years ago Plato made much the same observation, in that immortal passage in *Ion* which concludes: 'For the poet is a light and winged and holy thing, and there is no invention in him until he has been inspired and is out of his senses, and the mind is no longer in him: when he has not attained to this state, he is powerless and is unable to utter his oracles.'

II

A unity of the aesthetic and the moral should logically include the practical, for this philosophy of mine though general is not abstract or idealistic, but in the proper sense of the word, existential. It is made actual in deeds: in the deed which is the work of art, in the deed which is an inspired moral act. In this sphere again I have been led by logic and by history to the adoption of what is commonly regarded as an irrational doctrine: anarchism. I have written a separate book on this subject (*Poetry and Anarchism*) and here I intend to do no more than show the relation of this political doctrine to the general philosophy of life which I am now attempting to outline.

Anarchism, by its more philosophical exponents, has always been advocated as the *natural* order of society. But this ideal may be interpreted in more ways than one. An anarchist like Thoreau interprets it in a regressive sense. Mankind is one of the species that have to live on the products of the earth, and as a consequence we are intimately bound to that earth. We break the bond at our peril. Modern industrial civilization has broken the bond and we are therefore miserable and unhealthy. We must abandon such an artificial mode of life and return to the fields and the woods to live in direct contact with the soil from which we derive our spiritual no less than our bodily sustenance.

This doctrine is a literal interpretation of natural laws and might be best called 'naturism.' I do not dismiss it entirely: it expresses a fundamental law, one which we must take into account. But man, by virtue of his consciousness and intellect, has raised himself onto a plane higher than that of animal existence. He has elaborated his life in many directions; and these elaborations, which include his aesthetic perceptions and enjoyments, demand a mode of life which is correspondingly complicated. The highest achievements of humanity—a Greek tragedy, a Beethoven symphony, a novel by Flaubert or Henry James—are an expression of this complication and can only be appreciated fully in a highly civilized environment.

It is the quality of this civilization that we must control. The fact that we have not controlled it, by any universal standard, has led to the present chaos. Complication without order or principle is the very definition of chaos. There is now a general realization of this fact, and we only differ as to the nature of the order or principle which should be introduced. Those people who hide their lack of principle under the word realism can only conceive of a rational order of society invented by a minority (sometimes a minority of one) and imposed on the majority by force. Another party can only conceive of a moral order guaranteed by a super-natural sanction, and accepted not so much by reason as by goodness of heart. Such a moral order is the idea of a Christian society, and it is an idea which can still attract the mind as well as the heart. Its weakness is that it demands a voluntary emotional surrender, or alternatively an intui-tional recognition of absolute values: it cannot appeal to any external objective standard. The way which I consider the true way of thought is based on natural laws, but instead of giving them a literal interpretation, thereby reducing man-kind to the level of animal life, it allows an analogical in-terpretation—exactly the same kind of relationship that we have discovered between nature and art.

The laws of nature are physical laws: they can be grouped under such general terms as rhythm, proportion, balance, precision, economy, etc. These laws, which we derive from the observation of the process of the physical universe, must be applied to our social universe. To discover these laws and to live in accordance with them is a matter of individual discipline and conduct. It is possible to discover the laws by observation and measurement—the method of science. It is also possible to discover them by self-observation and medi-tation—the method recommended by Lao Tzu. To live in harmony with natural law—that should be our one suffi-cient aim. To create a society which enables the individual to pursue this aim is our political duty.

Such a society, itself reflecting the organic rhythms and balanced processes of nature, would give the individual the greatest degree of liberty consistent with a group organization. A group organization is itself a necessity only in order to guarantee this liberty. It will be a society that reduces the machinery of government to a minimum. It will safeguard itself against the rise of tyrants and will automatically destroy any form of authority which threatens the balance of its social metabolism. It will live and act as a communal unit whose only object is the provision of the material means of security and happiness. It will be governed by a final realization that happiness is only to be secured by the individual who is free to retire within himself and discover within himself that which the Taoists call the Way: the natural Truth. Such a society is anarchist.

It was noted that in aesthetics and morals, the physical analogy provided an escape from the prison of a closed system: a quantitative leap onto a new plane of consciousness or experience. But it is doubtful if the analogy can be pursued to this extreme on the social plane, which is the plane of the practical. Here we are limited by our economic and bodily needs, and the only escape from these is death, or that stasis of bodily functions practiced by Buddhist monks as a preparation for death. The final leap can only be into Nirvana, into the Heaven of the Christians, or into that more ideal and less individual immortality for which I have used the symbol of the Tree of Life. This ideal immortality, which is the only kind of which I myself can entertain an expectation, does not offer any consolation to those who, because they have not found the Way, identify their existence with their idiosyncrasies. But consolation is not necessary to the man who has shed his idiosyncrasies and accepted the laws implicit in the visible and material universe. Of such a man Santayana has said: 'The eternal has absorbed him while he lived, and when he is dead his influence brings others to the same absorption, making them, through that ideal identity with the best in him, reincarnations and perennial seats of all in him which he could rationally hope to rescue from destruction. He can say, without any subterfuge or desire to delude himself, that he shall not wholly die; for he will have a better notion than the vulgar of what constitutes his being. By becoming the spectator and confessor of his own death and of universal mutation, he will have identified himself with what is spiritual in all spirits and masterful in all apprehension; and so conceiving himself, he may truly feel and know that he is eternal.' *

III

Through all the mutations of these years I have relied on a weapon which I found in my hand as soon as I was compelled to abandon my innocent vision and fight against the despairs of experience. This weapon is adamantine and invincible, like the sickle which at the beginning of legendary time Earth gave to Cronus and with which he mutilated the divine father. The Furies were born from the drops of blood which fell in that fray. An adamantine sickle was also the weapon with which Hermes armed Perseus, and with which the head of Medusa was shorn off; and it was from

* *Reason in Religion* (1905), pp. 272-3.

that raw wound that the winged Pegasus sprang to life. Such a weapon is reason, which alone can slay despair, and cut the fetters of doubt and superstition which bind us to an Ethiopian rock. But as we wield this weapon, we find that it deals not only death, but life; and that new beings, the furies and the muses of our inspiration, gather round the carnage.

I called my first book of essays *Reason and Romanticism,* and the title was at once descriptive and prophetic. In this story of the growth of my mind, every advance has been due to the exercise of the faculty of reason; but that advance is not uniform, unimpeded. It abounds in deviations and contradictions: the opposed terms of a dialectical progression. The very bases of reason, the perceptions of an unclouded intellect, are continually being contradicted by the creative fictions of the imagination, by a world of illusion no less real than the reality of our quick awareness. It is the function of art to reconcile the contradictions inherent in our experience; but obviously an art which keeps to the canons of reason cannot make the necessary synthesis. Only an art which rises above conscious reality, only a transcendent or super-real art, is adequate. In this fact lies the final and inescapable justification of romantic art, and it is to the elucidation and illustration of this truth that I hope to devote my intellectual energy in the years that are left to me.